JOHN RAKESTRAW.
of Beer, Devonshire
"THE BOB ROY of the WEST".

MEMOIRS

OF

A SMUGGLER,

COMPILED FROM

His Diary and Journal:

CONTAINING

THE PRINCIPAL EVENTS IN THE LIFE OF

JOHN RATTENBURY,

OF BEER, DEVONSHIRE;

COMMONLY CALLED

"THE ROB ROY OF THE WEST."

" The story of his life,
From year to year, ev'n from his boyish days,
To the very moment that he tells it;
Wherein he speaks of most disastrous chances,
Of moving accidents by flood, by land,
And hair-breadth 'scapes from perils imminent,
Ev'n in the jaws of death."

"NIL DESPERANDUM."

---

*With a Portrait, and a correct Map of the Coast and Country Twenty
Miles each way round Beer.*

SIDMOUTH:

PRINTED, PUBLISHED, AND SOLD BY J. HARVEY.

LONDON:

LONGMAN AND CO.; WHITTAKER AND CO.; BALDWIN AND CO.;
HAMILTON AND CO.; BAGSTER AND SONS; TEGG AND SON;
TILT; AND RENSHAW AND KIRKMAN.

1837.

PREFACE.

————◆————

Few writings of the present day have been
more favourably received, or read with more eager
curiosity, than those of the *Autobiographist*. Nor
has this partiality been confined to the memoirs of
those who have directed the machinery of government, conducted the operations of fleets and armies,
or attained celebrity by their discoveries in science,
or their attainments in literature; it has extended
its fostering influence to the humblest individuals
whose characters have been marked by distin-
guishing peculiarities, or whose lives have been
diversified by remarkable events. At such a
period, it is presumed that the present work will
not be found destitute of attractions; especially
as the name of Rattenbury has long been familiar
to the public, and his exploits a theme of conversation from the little fishing cove of Beer (where
he was born) to the rocky shores of Vecta, and

from the islands surrounding the coast of Normandy
and Brittany to the remote promontory,

> "Where England, stretch'd toward the setting sun,
> Narrow and long, o'erlooks the western main."

Personal vanity, however, has had little influence
in drawing forth the manuscript from its hiding-
place. "The diary and journal of the smuggler"
would have remained locked up in the old chest
in his cottage till it had been transmitted by
death as a legacy to his descendants, had it
not been called forth by the solicitations of friends,
who are desirous of snatching his story from ob-
livion, and likewise of providing (by the profits
arising from the publication) the time-worn veteran
with some little resource against that period when
age shall have unstrung the arm of labour, and
when the infirmities of nature stand most in need
of support.

To the numerous and highly respectable list of
subscribers who have honoured this publication
with their support, the Old Smuggler begs to return
his most humble and sincere thanks.

MEMOIRS OF A SMUGGLER.

CHAPTER I.

I was born at Beer, in the county of Devon, in the year 1778. My father was by trade a shoemaker, but he went on board a man-of-war before I was born, and my mother never heard of him afterwards; she was, however, frugal and industrious, and by selling fish for our support, contrived to procure a livelihood without receiving the least assistance from the parish or any of her friends. Beer, where we resided, lying open to the sea, I was continually by the water-side; and as almost all I saw or heard was connected with that element, I early acquired a partiality for it, and determined, almost from my infancy, when I grew up, to be a sailor. When I was about nine years of age I asked my uncle to let me go fishing with him, to which he consented; and as there was another lad about the same age who went with us, we were continually trying to outvie each other in feats of skill and dexterity. I mention this circumstance, as I conceive it had a considerable effect in deciding the cast of my

B

character, and probably influenced many of the sub-
sequent events of my life. I continued with my uncle
for some time, but we afterwards separated in consequence of the following accident. Being one day at
Lyme, and having a quantity of fish to sell, he, accompanied by his son and a man that was with us,
went on shore for the purpose of disposing of them at
the market. I was left to take care of the boat, but
while they were absent I had the misfortune to lose
the rudder, in consequence of her getting aground.
When my uncle returned, and was informed of what
had happened, he flew into a violent passion, and beat
me with the end of a rope so severely that I resolved
to leave him as soon as I returned to Beer, which I
accordingly did. A few days after I met on the beach
a Brixham fisherman, who offered to take me as an
apprentice if I was inclined; I consented to go on
trial, and remained with him more than twelve months,
but he having a great many apprentices who were all
older than myself, they used me very roughly, and
made my situation very uncomfortable. One day,
having treated me worse than ordinarily, I determined
to endure it no longer, and a vessel belonging to Beer
being then at Brixham, I went to the captain, and
requested him to give me a passage back to my native
place, which he was so kind as to do. When I returned
home, finding to my great disappointment that I could
not get any employment, I proceeded to Bridport, and
engaged with the master of a vessel to go with him in
the coasting trade from Bridport to Dartmouth. I
remained, however, only a short time; for the man on

board being afraid of the press-gang, in consequence of the war which had broken out between England and France, left the vessel one morning about four o'clock, and not liking to continue on board alone, I was induced to accompany him, and returned again to Beer. On my arrival, I found that my uncle was busily engaged in entering men for privateering: this was a scheme then much talked of; and as nothing could better please my roving fancy than an enterprise of such a nature, I immediately entered, and with twenty-two others, men and boys, was conveyed in a small fishing sloop to Torquay, and put on board the Dover, commanded by Captain Mathews. For a few days we were all very actively employed in getting the lugger ready for sea, which was soon completed, for we were all very eager from the expectation of the prizes we should take, and the glory we should acquire. About the latter end of March, 1792, we proceeded on our first cruise off the Western islands; and even now, notwithstanding the lapse of years, I can recal the triumph and exultation which rushed through my veins as I saw the shores of my native country recede, and the vast ocean opening before me; I was like a bird which had escaped from the confinement of the cage, and obtained the liberty after which it panted. I thought on some who had risen from the lowest to the highest posts, from the cabin boy to the admiral's flag; I wished to make a figure on the stage of life, and my hopes and expectations were restless and boundless like the element around me. After having been six weeks at sea, without meeting with any thing worth relating, we put into Terceira, one of the Western islands, to take in provisions and water. We continued there four days, and then set out on another cruise, in the course of which we fell in with three American merchant ships laden with French goods; but their commanders contended that they were not lawful prizes, and they were suffered to proceed, though, as we were subsequently informed that these vessels were afterwards taken by English cruisers, I think it probable that there was some under-hand dealing between the American captains and our officers. We continued at sea six or seven weeks, part of the time on short allowance, and our provisions being nearly exhausted, we bore away again for Terceira to take in a fresh supply. In our voyage thither we spied a ship to our leeward, and it was agreed to bear down upon her, in order to ascertain what she was; when we came up with her we perceived that she carried English colours, and our captain ordered all hands to go aloft and to give her three cheers. But as we were preparing to do so, to our great surprise and alarm, the crew hauled down their English colours and hoisted French ones, and immediately fired two shots at us, one of which went through our jib, and the other between our fore and main-mast. As the French ship mounted twenty-six guns, resistance was out of the question, and escape impossible, and we were obliged quietly to submit to our fate. The captain then sent a boat alongside our vessel to take the crew on board his own ship, who were immediately ironed two and two, and sent down into the lower hold, where they found fifty other English prisoners

who had been captured out of a South Sea merchantman. Being a boy, I was ordered to stand by a gun
on the quarter deck, where I remained till five o'clock
in the evening, when I was sent below to join my companions. The next morning two other boys were
taken out of irons, and they, together with myself, were
appointed to attend to the prisoners, each having a
certain number allotted to his charge. Nothing could
be more truly deplorable than the situation of these
poor men, through the badness of their provisions and
the narrow space in which they were confined, inso-
much that though a boy, I often felt more for them
than for myself, and used to watch every opportunity
when the French sailors were on deck, to take all the
provisions I could procure, and carry them below to
my own shipmates, in order to mitigate their sufferings
as far as I was able. The French captain now directed
his course towards Bordeaux, and when we had been
steering for that port about a fortnight, two frigates
appeared in view. I was standing on the deck at the
time near the boatswain, and he supposed them to be
English, and being able to speak a little in that lan-
guage, then said to me, " Ah ! my boy, it is your turn
to-day, to-morrow it will be mine." As soon as I
could I went below, and told my comrades what we
had seen: they were overjoyed at the news; but alas !
their joy was of short duration, for a fog came on soon.
after, and by the next morning we had totally lost
sight of the frigates, which cast the greatest gloom over
the countenances of my companions. On the same
day, towards evening, we sailed up the Garonne, and

on the following day we entered the port of Bordeaux,
where we were taken on shore, and marched, ironed
two and two, to the prison of that place.

Such was the termination of an enterprise in which
we had all embarked with the greatest enthusiasm, and
thus visionary are the hopes of mortals! Instead of
returning to our native country laden with riches and
adorned with trophies, we were become, in the course
of a few months, unwilling sojourners in a strange
land; we had exchanged the sweets of freedom for the
galling fetters of captivity, and the pleasant homes of
our fathers for a foreign gaol, where some who had left
England in the bloom of youth, and full of all those
sanguine hopes which are connected with that gay
period, were destined at last to expire at a distance
from those they valued and by whom they were beloved,
without a parent or relative to watch by their sick
couch, to administer to their necessities, or even to
shed a tear over their graves. Our situation in captivity
was, however, far less deplorable than we could
reasonably expect, for the prison was airy and com-
modious, and the French people treated us with kindness and humanity. Not unfrequently, by order of
the keeper, I used to go to his house to fetch wine for
my fellow-prisoners; and, in the course of a few weeks,
I became such a favourite with him and his wife, that
I received great part of my provisions from their own
table, and was permitted every day to walk abroad in
the city, upon condition that I did not exceed the
time fixed for my return, which was seven o'clock
in summer. But notwithstanding this kindness and

partiality, and though I could not help being struck
with the novelties around me, such as the fine buildings,
extensive quay, and beautiful environs for which Bordeaux is so celebrated, yet I could not forget my native
land ; I felt a strange yearning after home, and was
continually endeavouring to contrive some plan for
making my escape. One evening, being engaged in
conversation with the master of an American vessel
with whom I had formed an acquaintance, I outstayed
my time, and on my return, the keeper of the prison
chid me very severely, and gave me two or three kicks.
After this period, I was not allowed to walk out again
without receiving an express permission or a written
order from the keeper. I now set all my wits to work
in order to carry the design which I had long meditated
into execution; and embracing an opportunity one day
when he was in the garden, I went to the sentry, and
showed him a ticket which I had received on a former
occasion, but which he had neglected to take: this he
received, as I had hoped, without examining the date,
and permitted me to pass.

As soon as I had made my escape, I hastened to a
coffee-house, where I found the American captain to
whom I have previously alluded, who, to my great joy,
agreed to take me on board his vessel, the George,
which then lay in Bordeaux harbour ; there I lay concealed for the space of a month, but not being able to
learn that any particular inquiry had been made after
me, and as I was afterwards conveyed on shore with
the crew, without meeting with any molestation, of
course my fears gradually subsided, and at last were

over, except at such times as I happened to offend
Captain Prowse, when he would threaten to deliver
me up, which used to terrify me not a little. We
remained at Bordeaux twelve months, in consequence
of an embargo on all foreign shipping, and as soon as
it was removed, having taken in a cargo of wine, &c.
we sailed for New York, where we arrived after a mid-
dling passage of forty-five days. There we discharged
our cargo, and the ship's company were paid off.

Captain Prowse, however, had taken a liking to me,
and offered to take me as an apprentice, but I was not
inclined to accept his proposal. I remained at New
York a few days, examining what was remarkable in the
place, and engaged in such amusements as it afforded;
and going by appointment to a house of public resort
in the city, to spend an evening with my late shipmates,
they each presented me with a dollar as a token of
their respect, and taking me on board a brig belonging
to the port, the captain of which agreed to give me
twenty dollars per month, to go with him as cook and
cabin boy; he also made me an advance of one month's
pay, to furnish myself with such clothes and necessaries
as I wanted.

Our first voyage was to Havre de Grace, where we
arrived after a passage of forty days; while there, the
captain had occasion to go to Paris, where he remained
more than a fortnight. During his absence, I heard
that there was an American merchantman, belonging
to Boston, called the Grand Turk; and hearing that she
was bound for London, and having a very great desire
to return to England, I went to the captain, and agreed

to go with him in the same situation as that which I had just left, for twelve dollars per month, with a further promise, that if I deserved more, he would give it to me. But to my great disappointment, however, instead of going to London, we proceeded to Copenhagen, where we arrived, after a passage of fourteen days. Here the captain discharged all the crew, except the mate and myself, and took a new one, consisting entirely of Danes, passing himself as supercargo, the first mate as passenger, and myself as servant to both. Nor should I forget to mention, that his conduct towards me was generous in the highest degree, for he advanced my wages to fifteen dollars per month, and put me before the mast, and after a very gratifying encomium on me, for diligence and activity, he assured me that I should never want a friend while I was with him, and continued to act as I had hitherto done. Our voyage was to Gottenburgh, where we remained five weeks, taking in a cargo of hemp, iron, potash and soap, with which we proceeded to Havre de Grace, but were driven into a creek near Crushing Sands in Norway, and obliged to continue there three months, in consequence of being weather-bound. The wind then becoming fair, we resumed our voyage, and arrived safe at Havre de Grace in ten days; then we discharged our cargo, and the supercargo paid me off, and told me that he was going as passenger to America, but he gave me a very handsome letter of recommendation, and we parted with mutual regret.

Having been paid in French paper-money, I was at a loss what to do, as I could not get it changed; I

therefore concluded to lay it out in clothes and fiddles,
with a view of disposing of them in barter the first
opportunity. Through the recommendation which I
had received, I now obtained a situation with another
American captain; and as the supercargo had given me
a very high character, he agreed to advance my pay to
sixteen dollars per month. Having taken in our cargo
of wine, we proceeded on our voyage, but the place of
our destination was unknown, as the captain did not
make it public, but after five days' sail, we arrived safe
at Guernsey; then I sold my clothes and fiddles, and to
my great joy met my uncle, who had come over with
bullocks for the English troops stationed there. When
we had discharged our cargo, I made application to
our captain for leave to go home, which he readily
consented to, on condition that I would return to him
again, when the time specified for my leave of absence
was expired. This affair being arranged, I went on
board the vessel with my uncle, and in the course of
two days arrived safe at Beer, where I had the pleasure
of seeing my mother, and the friends of my early
youth, who were all overjoyed to see me, and not a
little pleased with hearing me relate the adventures I
had met with.

At Beer, likewise, I found some of my old shipmates
who had been released from the prison at Bordeaux,
and found their way back to England; and we were
mutually interested in recording to each other the
various incidents which had occurred during the period
of our separation.

CHAPTER II.

I was now about sixteen years of age, and being fascinated with the charms of ease, after the sea of vicissitudes on which I had been tossed about, and the restless course in which I had been involved, I abandoned all thoughts of returning to Guernsey, and forfeited my promise to the American captain. This was an error, for as the engagement was a voluntary act, it ought to have been fulfilled ; this I mention for the benefit of those young persons into whose hands this narrative may fall, as a breach of social obligation is often attended with worldly inconveniences, and always with the loss of character. I remained at home about six months, part of which was occupied in fishing, but I found the employment very dull and tiresome after the roving life I had led ; and as the smuggling trade was then plied very briskly in the neighbourhood, I determined to try my fortune in it. I accordingly engaged in a small vessel which sailed out of Lyme to the Islands, in which I made a voyage with pretty good success, in the course of four months after which she was laid up. Being again in want of a situation, I applied to Captain Jarvis, and agreed to go with him in a vessel called the Friends, which belonged to Beer

and Seaton, but then lying in Bridport harbour. As
soon as she was rigged we proceeded to sea, but con-
trary winds coming on, we were obliged to put into
Lyme ; the next day the wind being favourable, at six
o'clock in the evening we put to sea again, and proceeded to Tenby, in Wales, where we were bound for
culm. At eight o'clock the captain set the watch, and
it was my turn to remain below ; at twelve I went on
deck, and continued till four, when I went below again,
but was scarcely dropped asleep, when I was aroused
by hearing the captain exclaim, " Come on deck, my
good fellow ! Here is a privateer, and we shall all be
taken." When I got up, I found the privateer close
alongside of us. The captain hailed us in English,
and asked us from what port we came, and where we
were bound. Our captain told the exact truth, and he
then sent a boat with an officer in her, to take all
hands on board his own vessel, which he did, except
myself and a little boy, who had never been to sea
before. He then sent his prize-master and four men
on board our brig, with orders to take her into the
nearest French port. When the privateer was gone,
the prize-master ordered me to go aloft and loose the
main-top-gallant sail. When I came down, I perceived
that he was steering very wildly, through ignorance of
the coast, and I offered to take the helm, to which he
consented, and directed me to steer south-east by south.
He then went below, and was engaged in drinking and
carousing with his companions. They likewise sent
me up a glass of grog occasionally, which animated
my spirits, and I began to conceive a hope not only of

escaping, but also of being revenged on the enemy.
A fog too came on, which befriended the design I had
in view; I therefore altered the course to east by
north, expecting that we might fall in with some English
vessel. As the day advanced, the fog gradually dis-
persed, and the sky getting clearer, we could perceive
land; the prize-master and his companions asked me
what land it was; I told them that it was Alderney,
which they believed, though at the same time we were
just off Portland. We then hauled our wind more to
the south until we cleared the Bill of the island; soon
after we came in sight of land off St. Albans: the
prize-master then again asked what land it was which
we saw; I told him it was Cape La Hogue. My companions then became suspicious and angry, thinking I
had deceived them, and they took a dog that had belonged to our captain, and threw him overboard in a
great rage, and knocked down his house. This I supposed to be done as a caution, and to intimate to me
what would be my own fate if I had deceived them.
We were now within a league of Swanage, and I per-
suaded them to go on shore to get a pilot: they then
hoisted out a boat, into which I got with three of them,
not without serious apprehension as to what would be
the event; but hope animated, and my fortunate genius
urged me on. We now came so near shore that the
people hailed us, and told us to keep further west. My
companions now began to swear, and said the people
spoke English: this I denied, and urged them to hail
again; but as they were rising to do so, I plunged
overboard, and came up the other side of the boat:

they then struck at me with their oars, and snapped a
pistol at me, but it missed fire. I still continued
swimming, and every time they attempted to strike me,
I made a dive and disappeared. The boat in which
they were now took in water, and finding they were
engaged in a vain pursuit, and endangering their own
lives and safety, with little chance of being able to
overtake me, they suddenly turned round, and rowed
away as fast as possible to regain the vessel. Having
got rid of my foes, I put forth all my efforts to get to
the shore, which I at last accomplished, though with
great difficulty. In the mean time the men in the boat
reached the brig, and spreading all their canvass, bore
away for the French coast. Being afraid that they
would get off with the vessel, I immediately sent two
men, one to the signal-house at St. Alban's, and another
to Swanage, to obtain all the assistance they could to
bring her back.

Fortunately, there was at the time in Swanage Bay
a small cutter, belonging to his majesty's customs,
called the Nancy, commanded by Captain Willis; and
as soon as he had received the information, he made
all sail after them; but I was not on board, not being
able to reach them in time, which was a great disappointment to me. The cutter came up with the brig,
about nine o'clock in the evening, and by retaking,
brought her into Cowes the same night, where the men
were put in prison. Captain Willis then sent me a
letter, stating what he had done, and advising me to go
as quickly as possible to the owners, and inform them
of all that had taken place. This I did without delay,

and one of them immediately set off for Cowes, when
he got her back by paying salvage. When the whole
transaction was over, I was not a little elated at the
part I had taken in it, but I never received any reward
for the service I had rendered, either from the owners,
or from any other quarter, though the affair was much
talked of at the time, and an account of it inserted in
the public papers. The owners having appointed
another captain in lieu of the former, who was taken a
prisoner to France, I proceeded with them to Cowes,
to rejoin the brig which had been re-captured.

  After I had been on board the vessel two days, a
lieutenant and his gang paid us a visit, with a view of
impressing men. When it came to my turn to be examined, I told him that I was an apprentice, and that
my name was German Phillips, (that being the name
of a young man, whose indenture I had for a protection.)
This stratagem however was of no avail with the keen-
eyed lieutenant, and he took me immediately on board
the Royal William, a guard ship, then lying at Spithead. I remained there in close confinement for a
month, hoping that by some chance or other, I might
be able to make my escape ; but seeing no prospect of
accomplishing my design, I at last volunteered my
services for the Royal Navy : if that can be called a
voluntary act, which is the effect of necessity, not of
inclination.

  And here I cannot help making a remark, on the
common practice of impressing seamen in the time of war.
Our country is called the land of liberty ; we possess
a just and invincible aversion to slavery at home and

in our foreign colonies, and it is triumphantly said that a slave cannot breathe in England. Yet how is this to be reconciled with the practice of tearing men from their weeping and afflicted families, and from the peaceable and useful pursuits of merchandise and commerce, and chaining them to a situation which is alike repugnant to their feelings and their principles? The impressed seaman in the day of battle, may sacrifice his resentment on the altar of patriotism, or, inspired by the example of others, he may perform miracles of valour; but in the ordinary scenes in which he is engaged, he will find his duties intolerably irksome, and will be ready to seize any opportunity that may present itself, of regaining liberty.

But to resume the thread of my story. As soon as I had agreed to enter, I was put on board a cutter, and went on a cruise off the islands of Guernsey, Alderney, &c. for a fortnight; after which we again returned to Spithead. Soon after our arrival there, I went on shore with the lieutenant and some of the crew, and watching an opportunity of stealing away from my companions, I met with my old master from Brixham, who was going to sail for that port on the following morning, and he took me on board his fishing smack, and the next day put me on shore at Portland, that I might be nearer home. When it was too late, I recollected that I had left my pocket-book behind me in the cutter, by which means the lieutenant found out my real name, and that the indenture which I had shown him was not my own. I now proceeded homeward with a quick but cautious step; on my way, I exchanged

a cap which I wore, with a young man, for his hat, and
avoiding Lyme, as I knew a gang was always kept there,
I went straight forward, and after a very fatiguing
walk, I got to Beer, without meeting with any interruption.   When I had been home for about a week,
some of the men from the cutter came to Lyme to
search after me.   On their way they met with the young
man who had my cap, and laid hold of him, saying,
that it was German Phillips's cap ; but they soon found
that he was not the person they were looking for, and
after various unsuccessful inquiries, they relinquished
the pursuit, and went back to Portsmouth.

CHAPTER III.

During the next six months I was occupied in
fishing and smuggling, but I had no great inclination
for either of those employments ; and about the same
time, the gang breaking up at Lyme, I went there in
the coasting and victualling trade, and remained there
till the beginning of the year 1800, when I entered my
twenty-second year. In February of the same year,
having been informed that there was a brig lying at
Topsham, that wanted hands, I immediately went to
the captain, whose name was Elson, and agreed with
him, for four pounds ten shillings per month. By the
latter end of March our vessel was ready for sea, and
having a fair wind, we proceeded on our voyage. We
put into Waterford for provisions, and soon after our
departure, the vessel sprung a leak, so that we were
obliged to return back again, and to take out all our
stores to get it repaired. And here I must not forget
to mention the kindness and humanity of Lord Rolle,
who being in that part of Ireland with his regiment at
the time, sent seventeen of his soldiers to assist us, by
which means our labour was greatly lightened and
accelerated.

The leak being stopped we put to sea again, and
after a three weeks' passage, arrived at St. John's,

which is the principal port in Newfoundland. There
we landed our passengers and part of our cargo; pro-
ceeding for Placentia, round Cape St. Mary's, we
discharged another part, and the remainder at Pacee,
in the same island, where our vessel was laid up. We
staid at Newfoundland three months, during which
time we were very busily employed in taking and curing
cod, in which we were pretty successful. Having
completed our arrangements in the month of November,
we took leave of that bleak spot, and proceeded to sea
with a cargo of prime fish, bound for Oporto, where we
intended to dispose of it.

When we were about four leagues from the place of
our destination, we had the misfortune to fall in with
a Spanish privateer, which chased us till ten o'clock
the next morning, when she came up to us, and we
were obliged to lie-to. The captain then sent some
of his people alongside of our vessel, who took out of
our crew all hands except myself and an Irish lad, and
sent a prize-master and ten men on board, with instructions to take our brig into Vigo, to which port the
privateer belonged. While in this situation, I was
continually forming schemes to get the upper-hand of
the enemy, which might have been done several times,
had the Irish youth been sufficiently awake to take the
different hints I gave; but finding my efforts fruitless, I
endeavoured to make myself as useful as I could, to
the Spanish officer who had the management of the
vessel, and with whom I became a great favourite; and
after being detained at sea, we arrived at Vigo in the
month of December.

The prize-master had been so much pleased with my behaviour, that when we came on shore, he took me into his own house to live with him, and recommended me in such strong terms to the owner of the privateer, that he presented me with thirty dollars, generously gave me my liberty, and lent me a mule to take me on my journey as far as Vienna. When I came there, I went to the British consul, and having been informed that if I asked him for assistance, he would detain me till some English man-of-war arrived, I simply asked for a pass, which he granted, and I then proceeded on my journey to Oporto, through a district abounding with the finest landscapes; but my thoughts were at this time so bent on returning home, and depressed by the misfortunes I had met with, that I could but very imperfectly enjoy the beauties of the surrounding country.

When I came to Oporto, I applied to the English consul there, for assistance. I found him a very kind-hearted man, and after I had given him my pass, and shown him the recommendation of the Spanish prize-master, he very humanely appointed me a house to live at, where I was also to be boarded free of expence, till I could find some opportunity of returning to England. I remained at Oporto for a few days, and having recovered from the fatigues of my journey, I went down on the quay, to look after a ship. As soon as I got there, I was hailed from a vessel by some one that I knew, and on going on board, to my great astonishment as well as joy, I saw my late captain and shipmates on the deck. Our surprise was mutual, but when the first emotions were subsided, the mystery was soon explained, for they told me that when the captain of the Spanish privateer arrived at the port, he very generously gave them their liberty, and put them on board a Danish brig, where I now found them, and after spending a very pleasant hour together, we all went on shore ; and I introduced my companions to the English consul, who received them very kindly, and gave them orders to go the house where I was stationed, with leave to remain there, till they could find some means of returning home.

The same evening, I went down to the quay alone, and found to my great joy, that there was a schooner lying there, bound for Guernsey. Having inquired the name of the merchant to whom she belonged, I went to him and related my story : he told me he could not make any regular engagement with me, but if I would go on board and assist in loading the vessel, he would satisfy me for my time, and he had no doubt we should come to a proper agreement. I accordingly followed his advice, and when we had laden the vessel with oranges, lemons, and other fruits belonging to the country, the captain returned, and after I had told him what had passed between the merchant and myself, and shown him the character I had received from the Spanish prize-master, he agreed to take me with him as his mate.

We then put to sea, and had fine weather for the first few days, after which heavy gales of wind came on, which greatly damaged our vessel, and compelled us to bear away for the coast of Ireland. When off Cape

Clear, we fell in with an Indiaman's mast and rigging,
but having no tools on board but an old axe whose
edge was very blunt, we could not cut any thing away.
When the weather cleared up, we saw a frigate about
a mile ahead of us, which we afterwards found to be
the Naiad, and the captain sent a boat alongside of
us to see what wreck we had fallen in with; and being
informed what it was, he sent his carpenter to our
assistance, who took the mast for firewood, and gave
us the rigging. We then put into Glendower in Ireland, and thence proceeded to Baltimore, where we
got a note of protest, and had the vessel repaired.
As soon as the weather became calmer, we again ventured to sea, and were out for three days, when tremendous gales came on again, and after being driven
about by the tumultuous elements in imminent peril of
our lives, with difficulty we reached the Cove of Cork.
We remained there for some days, and the weather
being fairer, again recommenced our voyage : having
been at sea five or six days with the wind in our favour
till we came off the Lizard Point, it then changed to
south-east, which obliged us to go into Mount's Bay ;
there the captain sold the rigging, and shared the
money amongst us, which proved very useful in providing necessaries we were in need of. We remained
at Mount's Bay for one week, and then sailed for
Guernsey, where we landed on the 25th of March,
without meeting with any particular accident. There
the captain sold the schooner, and having taken a
brig belonging to his brother-in-law, pressed me very
kindly to be his mate; but I had another object on

which I was much bent. I therefore declined this
advantageous offer which he made me, and finding
that there was a Weymouth packet then lying at
Guernsey, which was on the point of sailing, I went
as passenger in her, and arrived safe at Beer the following day, after having been absent for rather more
than twelve months.

CHAPTER IV.

BEFORE I set out on my last voyage, I had fixed my
affections on a young woman in the neighbourhood,
and it was agreed that our union should take place
immediately on my return. I now claimed the fulfil-
ment of this promise, and we were married on the 17th
of April, 1801. We then went to reside at Lyme, and
finding that I could not obtain any regular employment
at home, I again determined to try my fortune in
privateering, and accordingly engaged myself with
Captain Diamond, to go with him on board the Alert,
a lugger belonging to Weymouth, which was then
fitting out at Bridport for that purpose. Having completed our stores, in the month of May we set sail for
Alderney, and there took in our stock of wine and
spirits. We then steered to the Western islands, on a
cruise, in expectation of falling in with Spanish vessels,
and after being at sea for three months, put in at St.
Michael's, where we found in the roads a large ship
from Rio-de-la-Plata, laden with hides and tallow;
but to our great disappointment, after trying various
manœuvres to allure her out, that being a neutral port,
we were obliged to put to sea again, leaving her
behind.

The same day, we fell in with the Concord frigate, and our captain going on board, after having mentioned the circumstance, was informed that there was another ship from the river La Plata, that came out at the same time, at Fayal. The captain then went in to measure the distance, but found that we were within the limits.

We kept in company with the frigate for some days, and were parted during the night. After cruising for some time, we went into Fayal, to look after the Spanish ship, of which the captain of the Concord gave us information, and found her there; but, after having had recourse to every scheme in our power to decoy her out, and finding that all our stratagems were without effect, we relinquished the pursuit for a time, and put into Port-a-Pin close by. There we went on shore and drank with the Spaniards, and got the boatswain and four others to enter on board our vessel, which they had agreed to do; but, when they got on shore, they were found out, and taken prisoners. A few days afterwards, we went in again, and our captain spoke to the consul, who advised us to make off as quick as possible, as he was apprehensive that the Spaniards intended to fire on us. We accordingly took this advice, and went on another cruise; and on returning from it, put into St. Ubes in Portugal, to replenish our stock of provisions. The captain then asked us if we were inclined to go to sea for one month longer, and we agreed to do so, upon his promising to give us a month's wages in advance. After performing quarantine at St. Ubes, we took in our stock of provisions; and, leaving that port, continued cruising without any

c

success till Christmas day. The captain then mustered
all hands, and asked whether we were inclined to
abandon the undertaking, and return to England : to
this we readily gave our consent; and, putting the
helm hard-a-weather immediately, steered for home.

In the course of our voyage, we fell in with the
Alert, king's cutter; and our captain, going on board,
received a threat from the principal officer that he
would impress all his men ; to which he replied, that
he commanded such a set of resolute and desperate
fellows, that, if he attempted any such thing, they would
blow him and his vessel out of the water. When our
captain returned, having heard what had taken place,
we immediately put him below, and took charge of the
vessel ourselves; we then hoisted all the sail we could,
and got safe into Weymouth, on Sunday the 28th of
December, 1801. Immediately on my return, I went
to see my wife at Lyme, and remained at home about
four years, being principally engaged in piloting and
victualling ships. During this time, an American brig
came into the bay, and I went off to her with three
other men; but as soon as we were on the deck, the
prize-master ordered the people to bring up his pistols,
and detained me on board to pilot the brig into Weymouth, as there was not sufficient water to bring her
into Lyme. I performed this office very much to his
satisfaction, and at parting he gave me twenty guineas,
in consideration of the services I had rendered him.

On another occasion, I was sent for to Bridport, to
take charge of a vessel; and, the same night, a
lieutenant belonging to the Diamond frigate, in the

Greyhound cutter, came on board to impress men, who took me and put me in confinement, and a man over the scuttle to keep me down, while he overhauled other vessels that were lying there. When he was gone, I said to the man who was put to guard me, " I will give you a guinea if you will let me come up," which offer he accepted. As soon as I came upon deck, I jumped overboard, but the man giving an alarm, the gang surrounded and re-captured me, after which they carried me in triumph to the boat. I now employed my wits in endeavouring to find out some way of escape; and, when daylight came, I said to the lieutenant, "If you will go on shore, I will show you where there are some fine young fellows :" to this he readily agreed. We then went on shore, and I pointed out a public-house to him; but, not finding any there, he began to suspect that my design was to get free, and ordered me down into the boat with the rest of his men. As we were going there I saw my wife coming towards me, and entreated him to let me stop a moment to speak to her; this he gruffly refused, and in an angry tone, again ordered me forward to the boat. As soon as I got on board, I made a start through the water, and up the town; he followed me with nine of his men, upon which my wife collared him, and he threw her down; a scuffle then ensued, in which the towns-people took part, while I made my escape, and got clear off.

CHAPTER V.

AFTER this adventure, I went to reside at Beer, and made a great many trips in smuggling, several of them attended with the most complete success; but, at other times, I had the mortification to see my property captured, through the vigilance of those officers who, like harpies, were continually hovering round the shore, and looking out for prey. Among the foremost of these was the lieutenant of the Greyhound, from whose clutches I had so recently escaped. One instance in which I very narrowly eluded his pursuit was attended with such extraordinary, and at the same time ludicrous circumstances, that I will insert it here, as I think it will amuse the reader. Being at Weymouth, and finding that he was endeavouring to pounce upon me, I took refuge in a public-house, with the landlord of which I was well acquainted. But having obtained intelligence of my lurking-place, about two o'clock in the morning he paid us a visit, and roused us from the arms of sleep, swearing that if the landlord did not come down and open the door, he would fire at him through the window, and force an entrance. Immediately on his giving the alarm, I climbed up the chimney, and remained there about an hour, while he was

narrowly inspecting the premises. On his departure,
when all was quiet, I came down, covered with soot all
over, making a most dismal appearance; and I likewise
found I had bruised myself considerably, through the
narrowness of the aperture in which I had been confined, and the difficulty of breathing in it; but I now
triumphed over the sense of pain itself, in the exultation
which I experienced at having once more escaped out
of the clutches of this keen-eyed lieutenant and inde-
fatigable pickaroon.

Wearied out by the incessant pursuit of my enemies,
and finding that I was followed by them from place to
place like the hunted stag by the hounds, or the worried
bird by the sportsman, I at last determined, with a
view of getting rid of them, again to go privateering.
Accordingly I shipped myself on board the Unity
cutter, a privateer vessel then fitting out for Weymouth,
commanded by Captain Head. About February, 1805,
we proceeded to sea, and after touching at Alderney,
to take in our stock of spirits and other refreshments,
we steered our course towards Madeira, Teneriffe, &c.,
in the hope of falling in with prizes: we continued
cruising in this direction for about ten weeks, without
meeting with any success. We then put into St.
Michael's for water, &c.; and, while we were in the
roads, the captain gave part of the crew (consisting of
the second commander and fifteen men,) leave to go
on shore for a day's pleasure. After spending the day
together in the utmost concord and conviviality, about
seven o'clock in the evening, being the time appointed
for our return, we put off from shore; but, when we

got alongside of the cutter, our commanding officer
made a jump and upset the boat, by which means we
were all hands precipitated into the water. A dreadful
scene then ensued, for it was dark, and we were all
every moment expecting a watery grave. The accidents
which have so often happened in such situations, of
drowning men laying hold of one another, instantly
occurred to my mind, and I swam away as fast I could,
to avoid the danger. When I thought all was quiet, I
swam alongside the vessel; and while I was doing so,
I fell in with a man who was much exhausted, but still
clinging to an oar, by which he was endeavouring to
support himself. I gave him all the assistance that
was in my power, and finally succeeded in getting on
board with my companion. Some other of my shipmates had the good fortune to do the same, among
whom were two men completely spent with fatigue,
who had taken in so much water, that two or three
days elapsed before they perfectly recovered. We
then mustered the men, and upon calling over their
names, found with regret that two were missing. Having
no boat, we could not seek after them, and we never
saw them any more. Poor fellows! they left the ship
in the morning, full of gaiety: they had been spending
the day in festive amusements, and in the evening the
sea was their winding-sheet.

The next morning, the Portuguese succeeded in
getting the boat, and brought her off to us; but she
was so shattered that we were obliged to have her
repaired before we put to sea again. After having
been engaged in another cruise for about eight weeks,

without any success, we steered for the beautiful island of Madeira, where we found another privateer belonging to Guernsey, whose captain told us that the day before, several of his men had been impressed by Le Egyptien frigate, which then lay in sight; this struck such a panic into our people that they all went on shore, except myself and four others. The frigate, however, did not long remain in the roads; and, after her departure, having got our men on board, and such articles of refreshment as we stood in need of, we immediately took our course for England. In our voyage homeward, we saw several men-of-war, but our vessel being a swift sailer, none of them could get up with us.

In the month of August, 1805, we arrived at Beer, where we put on shore all those who were afraid of being impressed; and, having completed my voyage, in consequence of the ill success I had met with, I determined never again to engage in privateering, a resolution which I have ever since kept, and of which I have never repented.

PART II.

CHAPTER I.

On my return home, I engaged ostensibly in the trade of fishing, but, in reality, was principally employed in that of smuggling, in the course of which I met with many extraordinary adventures, and all the variety of fortune that usually attends that precarious line of life. I have set down these occurrences in their chronological order; and the relation of them, together with the events to which they gave rise, will form the most considerable part of the ensuing narrative.

My first voyage was to Christchurch, in an open boat, where we took in a cargo of contraband goods; and, on our return, safely landed the whole.

Being elated with this success, we immediately proceeded to the same port again; but on our way, we fell in with the Roebuck tender: a warm chase then ensued; and, in firing at us, a man, named Slaughter, on board the tender, had the misfortune to blow his arm off. Eventually, the enemy came up with and captured us; and, on being taken on board, we found the captain in a great rage in consequence of the accident

which had occurred; and he swore he would put us all
on board a man-of-war. Soon after, he hailed a boat
belonging to the government service, to come alongside, in order to put this threat into execution, but she
passed on, without paying any attention. He then
got his own boat out to take the wounded man on
shore; and, while this was going forward, I watched
an opportunity, and stowed myself away in her, unknown to any person there. I remained without being
perceived, amidst the confusion that prevailed; and,
when they had reached the shore, I left the boat, and
got clear off. The same night, I went alone in a boat
that I had borrowed, alongside the tender, and rescued
all my companions; we likewise brought three kegs
of gin away with us, and landed safe at Weymouth,
from whence we made the best of our way home. This
I regarded as a great achievement, and perhaps no
naval or military chief ever more proudly exulted in
the wreaths of victory with which fortune had crowned
him.

The same winter, I made seven voyages in a smuggling vessel which had just been built; five of them
were attended with success, and two of them turned
out failures, and she was then laid up.

In the spring of the year 1806, I went to Alderney,
where we took in a cargo; but, returning, fell in with
the Duke of York cutter, in consequence of getting
too close to her boat in a fog without perceiving her.
Being unable to make our escape, we were immediately
put on board the cutter, and the crew picked up some
of our kegs which were floating near by, but we had

previously sunk the principal part. As soon as we were secured, the captain called us into his cabin, and told us that if we would take up the kegs for him, he would give us our boat and liberty, on the honour of a gentleman. To this proposal we readily agreed; and, having pointed out where they lay, we took them up for him. We then of course expected that the captain would have been us good as his word; but, instead of doing so, he very disgracefully departed from it, and a fresh breeze springing up to the eastward, we steered away hard for Dartmouth. When we came alongside the castle, the cutter being then going at the rate of six knots, I jumped overboard; but having a boat in her stern, they immediately lowered her down with a man, to whom the captain exclaimed, "If you do not bring him back, you shall go in his stead." I succeeded, however, in getting on shore, and concealed myself among some bushes; but two women who saw me go into the thicket, inadvertently told the boat's crew where I was, upon which they immediately retook me, and I was carried on board quite exhausted with fatigue and loss of blood, for I had cut myself in different places. When I came on board, I was in such a pickle that my own shipmates could not help laughing at me; and the captain, being completely aggravated, exclaimed to me, "I will put you on board a man-of-war, and send you to the East Indies;" to which I replied, by calling him an "old rascal," an expression which only tended to sharpen his anger still more.

As soon as the cutter was brought to an anchor, the captain went on shore; about an hour afterwards, a

lieutenant and his gang came on board from Dartmouth;
and said to the chief mate, " What a fine set of young
lads you have here!" and afterwards expressed a wish
to take us on shore with him ; to which our commanding
officer said, he could not consent during the absence,
and without the orders of the captain. The following
morning, the captain came on board, and took us all on
shore with him to Dartmouth ; there we were taken by
the cutter's people and an escort of constables to the
town-hall, and tried by the magistrates, who sentenced
us to pay a fine of one hundred pounds each, to go on
board a man-of-war, or to gaol, which we pleased.
After a very short consultation, we unanimously agreed
to the last condition, upon which we were all crammed
into a most deplorable hole, in which they were accustomed to confine vagrants. We remained there till
about six o'clock in the evening, when, being heartily
sick of a place that seemed to have been constructed
after the model of the Black Hole at Calcutta, I told
my companions that they might do as they pleased,
but that I was determined to go on board ; upon hearing this, they all agreed to follow my example, and,
having signified our wish, we were liberated from our
doleful confinement, and entered for the Kite brig,
then lying in the Downs. The same night, we were
removed to the Safeguard brig, which then lay in
Dartmouth roads. The next morning, the captain,
who had been absent, came on board, and calling us
up, asked us a few questions relative to our case, after
which, we told him that the captain of the cutter had
promised us four gallons of gin ; upon which, he im-

mediately went on board the cutter himself, and got them for us, giving them to the steward, with a charge to let us have two bottles at a time. The first two were then given to us; and, after drinking them, we all began to be pretty merry.

I then went on the quarter-deck, and asked the captain if he would allow me to go on board the cutter, saying, that I had some private communication to make to the captain; to this he readily consented, little imagining at the time, that I was forming a scheme for regaining my liberty. A boat was then lowered down; and he sent the master of the ship and four men with me off to the cutter.

When I came on board, they asked me to take something to drink; and, while I was doing so, I saw the master drinking likewise with some officers, and busily engaged in conversation on the quarter-deck; I also noticed that the main-sail had been partly hoisted, so that neither he nor the boat's crew could command a prospect of the shore. I then went forward, and looking round, saw that the coast was clear, when I immediately jumped down on the bobstay, and seeing that a little boat was approaching, I held up my finger to the man that was in it, as a signal to come and drop under the bows; this he did with great celerity, and, in less than five minutes, landed me at King's Wear, opposite to Dartmouth. As soon as it was accomplished, I gave the fisherman a pound note, for the assistance he had rendered me, and made the best of my way to Brixham, which is five miles distant. When I had walked, or rather run, the first mile, I

borrowed a horse from a farmer, on which I rode the
remaining four; and, as soon as I arrived there, I hired
a fishing smack, in which I got safe home. I afterwards found that the people at King's Wear supposed
that I must have been at Brixham before my escape
was detected; and likewise that several marines and
sailors were dispatched different ways in search after
me, who to the great mortification of my enemies,
returned just as they went; but I found that the officers
were very suspicious of my companions who were left
behind, and kept a very sharp look-out upon them.

CHAPTER II.

Soon after my return home, I purchased part of a galley, in which I made several successful voyages; and on one occasion, very narrowly escaped being taken: for, returning from the island of Alderney one night, we fell in with a custom-house boat, by whom we were chased, and the crew fired at us; but when they came up, we told them that we belonged to the Alarm lugger, and the darkness befriending us, the stratagem succeeded, and we got off.

Having had the misfortune to lose the galley at sea, I went in the month of June, with two other men, in an open boat, to Alderney, to get kegs; but in our voyage home, about half-channel over, we were chased by the Humber sloop, commanded by Captain Hill, who took myself and my companions, boat and all, and carried us into Falmouth, to which port the sloop belonged. As soon as we arrived there, we requested to be sent on shore, to receive our trial; but the captain refused, and took us again to sea with him, on a cruise, so that it was not till the 20th of July, that we were brought before the magistrates at Falmouth, who having heard the case, committed us to prison.

As it was too late in the afternoon when the trial was

over, the captain took us for that night on board his
ship, and in the morning, when we came on shore, we
were put into two post-chaises, with two constables to
take care of us, and were sent forward to Bodmin gaol.
As our guards stopped at almost every public-house we
came to, towards evening they became pretty merry;
and taking advantage of this circumstance, I was determined to find some place for making my escape.
Accordingly, when we came to the Indian Queen, (a
public-house, a few miles from Bodmin,) while the
constables were taking their potations, I bribed the
drivers not to interfere. Having finished, the constables ordered us again into the chaise, but we refused.
A scuffle ensued. One of them collared me, some
blows were exchanged, and he fired a pistol, the ball of
which went off close by my head. My companion
in the mean time, was engaged in encountering the
other constable, and he called upon the drivers to aid
and assist, but they said it was their duty to attend to
the horses. We soon got the upper-hand of our
opponents, and seeing a cottage near, I ran towards '
it, and the woman who occupied it was so kind as to
show me through her house into the garden, and to
point out the road. I made the best of my way
forward; and when I had proceeded about a mile, on
looking back, I perceived a man following me, upon
which I crept into a ditch for concealment. When
the person came up, he hailed me by name, and I found
it was my fellow-prisoner, who had made his escape
likewise, through the aid of the woman at the cottage.
We then went on our journey together, and towards

evening, we met with a party of men, who were
smugglers like ourselves; and having told them our
adventures, they behaved very handsomely to us, and
took us the same night to a place called Newkey,
where we slept. The next morning we got up very
early, and hired three horses for Mevagissey, the landlord going with us to take them back. Here we had
the good fortune to fall in with a friend, who lent us
ten pounds, our money being almost exhausted. We
hired a boat, which took us to Budleigh Salterton, that
being the most convenient place to land at, as the wind
was easterly. On the following day we walked on
together, and in the evening, to our great joy, arrived
safe at Beer.

CHAPTER III.

THE latter end of July, I went again in an open boat
to the island of Alderney, where we took in a cargo of
contraband articles, with which we arrived safe home.
About the same time, I met with an old captain, with
whom I had been for several years acquainted, who
was going to leave his vessel for another; and in consequence of his recommendation to the owners, I was
appointed to succeed him.   This vessel was called the
Trafalgar, and my first voyage in her was to Newport for
coals, which we completed in seven days; we next
went to Leith for a cargo of culm, which we accomplished in eighteen days.   I then received orders to get
a standing bowsprit, and to steer for the islands, for the
purpose of smuggling.   I made five successful voyages
to Alderney, but returning the last time, when nearly
arrived at the place of our destination, we fell in with
a gang-boat, commanded by Lieut. Millar, before I
was aware, through the haziness of the weather.   As
soon as I perceived the danger we were in, I ordered a
man to the mast-head, to loose the gaff-topsail, and
having a fine breeze, we bore away; but she afterwards
came up again almost alongside of us; then I luffed
the vessel, to keep her to wind, and he did the same,

but during the chase his mast went overboard, by which means we got clear off, and sunk our goods.

We then steered again for Alderney; and when I landed, I sent a pilot off, to take charge of the vessel, with instructions to sail round about the island, while I got the goods ready to put on board; we were not however able to load the vessel as soon as I expected, through the revenue officers keeping a very sharp look-out, in consequence of which, they took the vessel out to sea again, leaving me ashore. They afterwards attempted to put in at the pier, but found they could not, without letting go the anchor; which they did in such an awkward bungling manner, notwithstanding the directions which I gave them from the shore, that at last they ran the vessel on the rocks. I immediately got a boat and pushed off; but when I came on board, I found the vessel in a most deplorable state, the sea breaking over her, and her bottom striking with tremendous force against the shingles, so that I found it was impossible that she could hold together many minutes. I then ran below, and snatched up my pocket-book, leaving my watch, clothes, and other articles behind, and having jumped into the boat with my companions, we had scarcely time to get clear, when the vessel went asunder, separating into two parts, her lower from her upper works. As soon as I reached the shore, I mustered all the hands I could, and by inde-fatigable exertion, we succeeded in recovering the greater part of the materials from the wreck.

Four days after this disaster, I put the goods and the men on board another vessel, and sent them home,

but during the night they fell in with the Liberty brig
and Pluto sloop of war, who took them prisoners, and
also captured the cargo. The same day, having settled
my business in the island, I went on board another
vessel, which I had hired, and laden with contraband
goods, and was chased by the same king's ships, but
by management in sailing got off, and made a good
voyage. A few months afterwards, I went with three
other men in an open boat to the islands, and we made
two good voyages. We then bought an eight-oared
boat, which had belonged to the Alarm cutter, and been
condemned at the custom-house, in which we succeeded
very well.

In the fall of the same year, we went to St. Helen's,
and bought a small vessel, called the Lively; but
crossing the channel, we met with a sad disaster, for
we were chased by a French privateer, and the man at
the helm was shot. The privateer afterwards came up
with us; but the captain was so affected by the occurrence which had taken place, that he generously
gave up the vessel. We afterwards made three voyages
in her, but she was so leaky, that it was accomplished
at the extreme hazard of our lives. Being fearful of
venturing again in her, in this state, we had her hauled
upon the beach, and stripped to undergo repairs. We
then bought a vessel called the Neptune, in which we
made three prosperous voyages; but on the fourth she
was wrecked while going into Alderney, in one of the
most violent gales of wind from the north, that I ever
remember.

On this melancholy occasion, twenty-three vessels

broke from their moorings, and only three held on,
viz., a custom-house cutter, a merchant brig, and a
fishing smack, which rode out the gale. It was indeed
a shocking and tremendous spectacle, to see so many
vessels drifting about, and their crews at their wits'
end; no person being able to help the other, or daring
to venture from land, to give them the least assistance.
Our vessel was driven on shore, and went to pieces;
while I and my companions escaped a watery grave by
jumping from vessel to vessel, till we got into one, in
which we waited till the tide went back, and the
violence of the tempest subsided. There was a Brixham vessel which came off better than the rest, and a
fishing smack from the same port went into Alderney
in the midst of the gale. With the captain of the last,
I made an agreement to take myself and my goods to
the main land; which he did, and I got home after all,
without meeting with any further disaster, and saved
the cargo.

Misfortunes, it is said, seldom come alone, and the
truth of this adage we were doomed to experience; for
the vessel, which I have before mentioned, that was
hauled up on the beach, having been repaired, was at
sea in this violent gale, and put into Brixham; when
the officers, suspecting what she was, went on board
and seized her; and I, being bondsman for her, in the
sum of one hundred and sixty pounds, was arrested for
the same, a few months afterwards, and was obliged to
pay it, without being able to obtain the smallest mitiga-
tion. This, however, was a great shock to my circumstances.

Not long after this disaster, I bought part of a twelve-oared boat, which was fifty-three feet keel, and sixty feet aloft. In her we made a voyage to Alderney, and took in a cargo; but, on her return, when we had scarcely been two hours at sea, we fell in with two king's cutters, that had been sent to look for us, viz., the Stork, Captain Emys, and the Swallow, Captain Ferres. As soon as we perceived them, we veered off, and got under the French land; but, finding this manœuvre would not do, we altered our course for England. A very arduous chase then ensued, the result of which was for a long time doubtful; but, notwithstanding our utmost efforts, about six o'clock in the evening, the Swallow came up with us, while the Stork was about the third of a league behind, picking up the tubs which we had thrown overboard; and as soon as the Swallow came alongside, all the persons in our boat, except myself and two others, rowed off in her, and made their escape. As soon as I and my companions were taken on board the Swallow, the captain asked me for my papers, which I delivered up to him; he then went off in his boat to the other cutter, and soon afterwards returned with captain Emys, who took me on board with him; and, being a man of courteous manners, though I was a smuggler and his prisoner, he behaved towards me with great kindness, and even invited me into his cabin, where I both ate and drank with him. The next day, having picked up our tubs, they proceeded to Weymouth roads, where my companions sent a friend off in a boat, with a letter to me; but the captain of the Stork

would not allow it to be delivered, and ordered
me below. The succeeding morning, about the dawn
of day, the two cutters with their prize, set out for
Cowes; and, soon after their arrival there, a lieutenant
and his gang came on board; when the captain said
to me, "Rattenbury, I am going to send you on board
a man-of-war, and you must get clear how you can."
To which I replied, "Sir, you have been giving me roast
meat ever since I have been on board, and now you
have run the spit into me." I was then put on board
the Royal William, the ship from which I had before
made my escape; there I found a great many smugglers
with whom I was acquainted, but none of the officers
seemed to have any recollection of me, though I was
on board for a fortnight. Soon after, I, and all the
other smugglers, were drafted on board the Resistance
frigate, Captain Adams; and the next evening set
sail from Portsmouth for Ireland: we were at sea eight
days, when we arrived at Cork.

I now thought that it was high time to form some
plan for regaining my liberty; and, after being there
four days, I told my scheme to an Irish bumboat-man,
who engaged to come to the ship's buoy, when I was
to swim off to him; and, if he got me safe on shore,
I agreed to give him seven guineas. The man was
punctual to his appointment, but the marines kept
such a strict look-out, that it was impossible for me to
accomplish my design; and, seeing little prospect of
being able to do so, I determined to keep my eyes
open, and to seize the first opportunity of getting clear
in some other way.

The next day, being Tuesday, the ship's launch came alongside, to take in casks for the purpose of getting water; and, while the first lieutenant was scolding a midshipman because he was not sufficiently expeditious in getting them on board, I jumped into the boat with a cask before me, and taking an oar in my hand, assisted with others in rowing to the shore. When we came there, we found another boat which was also taking in water; and, as this created some delay, the midshipman said that he would take us all to a public-house, and get some whiskey. I got out with the rest, and soon after, stole away, unperceived by any one, and ran four miles into the country. There I fell in with a very civil kind-hearted woman, to whom I disclosed so much of my story as I deemed necessary; she then took me to a farm-house, where I was treated very hospitably, and the farmer was so kind as to send his son to the Cove of Cork, to collect all the news that he could; when he returned, he said that the whole place was in a kind of alarm respecting the captain of the smugglers having made his escape, and that marine officers and their men had been sent to search every public-house, with a view of apprehending and bringing me back.

Upon receiving this intelligence, the same evening I hired a gig, and set out for Youghal, where I arrived the following morning about day-break. I then went to the harbour to inquire for a vessel for England, and had the good fortune to find one bound for Weymouth. I went on board, and met the mate, who introduced me to the captain; and, as he had a brother who was

a fellow-smuggler, with whom I had long been acquainted, we soon came to an agreement. The captain
behaved very kindly towards me, and I went the same
day and dined with him and all the masters of vessels
that were there, two officers of the royal navy being
of the party. We spent three hours together. I passed
for the captain of a vessel. The same evening we set
sail; and, after being at sea three days, got off Start
Point. The captain then put me on board a boat
bound for Brixham, and there I found another from
Beer, where I arived safe at four o'clock on Sunday
morning, to the great joy of myself, my wife, and
family; having performed the whole expedition, as the
reader may trace by referring to the dates from my
escape from Cork, in six days.

CHAPTER IV.

NOT long after my return home, I made an agreement with four French officers, who had made their
escape from the prison at Tiverton, to take them to
Cape La Hogue, for which I was to receive one hundred pounds. They came to Beer, and I concealed
them in the best manner I was able, in a house near
the beach, where I supplied them with such provisions
as they wanted. But a vigilant inquiry was com-
menced; their steps were traced, and the place of their
retreat discovered. The next morning, there was a
special warrant out against myself and five others, who
were connected with the affair, and the constables came
to my house, while I was up-stairs considering how I
had best act. Finding that my companions had ab-
sconded, and being captain of the boat, I immediately
surrendered myself up to them. I was then taken before
the magistrates, where I found the French gentlemen
in custody. They were examined through the medium
of an interpreter, but their replies were cautious, and
they said very little that could tend to implicate me in
the transaction. My turn then came; and, in reply to
the questions from the bench, I briefly stated that I
was engaged to take the gentlemen to Jersey, of which

island I understood that they were natives. A lieutenant of the sea-fencibles being in the room, asked me
if I did not know a native of Jersey from a Frenchman;
to which I was going to have replied, but my attorney,
who was present, said that this was a question which
he had no right to prefer, and which I was not bound
to answer. The magistrates then conversed together;
and, after a little consultation, dismissed me, with a
gentle admonition to go home, and not engage in any
similar transaction for the future.

A short time after the above, a lieutenant of the sea-
fencibles, whose name was Durall, went to my house
with a constable, to apprehend me as a deserter from
his majesty's navy. I happened, however, to see them
go in; and, judging what was the object of their visit,
made my escape round the cliffs, and remained from
home, till I thought the storm which had threatened to
destroy my domestic peace had blown over.

Soon after this occurrence took place, I bought a
vessel for smuggling, in which I made three successful
voyages to Alderney; and on my return from the last,
thinking all was safe, I went on shore with a few friends
to spend an hour at a public-house. In the same
room were a sergeant and several privates belonging to
the South Devon militia, and also some horse-soldiers,
amounting in the whole to nine or ten in number;
who, after drinking two or three pots of beer, the sergeant, whose name was Hill, having heard my name
mentioned by some of my companions, went out with his
men, and soon after they returned again, having armed
themselves with swords and muskets. The sergeant

then advanced towards me, and said, "You are my
prisoner; you are a deserter, and must go along with
me." For a moment I was much terrified, knowing
that, if I was taken, I should in all probability be
obliged to go through the fleet; and this wrought up
my mind to a pitch of desperation. I endeavoured,
however, to appear as cool as possible; and, in answer
to his charge, I replied, "Sergeant, you are surely
labouring under an error; I have done nothing that
can authorize you in taking me up, or detaining me;
you must certainly have mistaken me for some other
person." In this manner, I contrived to draw him into
a parley; and, while it was going on, I jumped into
the cellar. I then threw off my jacket and shirt, to
prevent any one from holding me; and, having armed
myself with a reaphook, and a knife which I had in
my pocket, I threw myself into an attitude of defence
at the entrance, which was a half-hatch door, the lower
part of which I shut, and then declared that I would
kill the first man who came near me, and that I would
not be taken from the spot alive. At this, the sergeant
was evidently terrified, but he said to his men, "Soldiers,
do your duty, advance and seize him;" to which they
replied, "Sergeant, you proposed it: take the lead,
and set us an example, and we will follow." No one,
however, offered to advance, and I remained in the
position which I have described, for four hours, holding
them at bay. Not knowing how to act, the sergeant
at last sent to Lieutenant Durall; but before he arrived,
some women ran into the house, with a story that there
was a vessel drifted ashore, and a boy in danger of

being drowned. This tale they told in such a natural
manner, that it attracted the attention of the sergeant
and his men; and, while they were listening and making
inquiries about it, I jumped over the hatch, and rushed
through the midst of them, without their being able to
lay fast hold of me, in consequence of the precaution
which I had taken to lay aside my clothes. I then ran
towards the beach, and some men got me into a boat,
and conveyed me on board the vessel, where I immediately hoisted the colours.

By this time, Lieutenant Durall was come down to
the beach ; and, seeing the colours flying, asked what
was the cause; to which some bystanders replied, that
it was only a freak of Rattenbury's, who had escaped
from the soldiers, and got on board his vessel, and
they supposed had done it by way of triumph. Upon
hearing this, he flew into a great rage, and told the
soldiers, that if they could take and bring me to him,
besides the deserting money, he would give them two
guineas out of his own pocket. I took care, however,
to keep myself close on board ; and a friend desired
me to put into Lyme, and said that he would be sure
to keep a sharp look-out, and always inform me when
I was likely to be in the way of danger. I then made
a voyage to Alderney in two days, there and back
again, and saved the cargo; and afterwards several
others with similar success, liking to put into Lyme,
as often as possible, as I had several good friends
there.

Having slept one night at Lyme, I went down early
in the morning to see how the vessel lay, being appre-

hensive about the weather. Upon looking round, I
saw that the sky looked very dark and angry, and that
there was every appearance of a heavy gale coming
on. Soon after I heard the report of a gun, and then
another ; and on jumping upon a wall to have a wider
view, I saw a brig in the offing, with her colours up, as
a signal of distress.   I then got a boat, and three men,
and put off to her immediately, and on reaching her,
found that it was the Linskill transport, having on
board several officers, and part of the eighty-second
regiment.   As soon as we came alongside, the captain
begged us to take them into some harbour, saying, that
he was a stranger to the coast, and that they were
under the most serious apprehension of losing the
vessel, and their lives ; to which I replied, that I would
use every effort in my power to save both. We then
went on board, and I asked the captain what water he
drew, and finding that it was eleven feet, I said, that it
was impossible for me to take them into Lyme, as it
was then neap tides, and the gale was rapidly coming
on.   At the same time, another transport came into the
bay, almost close to us, upon which the officers entreated me not to leave them, but to take the vessel
into some other port.   We then sent a boat to the other
vessel, and directed them to keep close after us; and
then made all the canvass we could. When we got clear
outside Portland, we fell in with an East-Indiaman,
that asked for assistance, the gale being then very
violent ; but we were unable to afford them any, and
we heard no more of her fate. Through the goodness
of Divine Providence, we at last weathered this tre-

mendous storm; and when we appeared out of danger,
the officers being profuse in their acknowledgments
of gratitude, for the service I had rendered them, I
ventured to open my story, by stating what had occurred,
how my enemies were in search of me, and what
trouble I was in. They heard the whole with great
attention, and upon asking their advice, they recommended me, as soon as they got on shore, to get a
hand-bill printed, describing what I had done in their
behalf, and presented me with a guinea to defray the
expenses. I carried the transport into the Needles,
when she took another pilot. At parting, the captain
gave me twenty guineas for my pilotage; and I left the
vessel amidst the highest commendations of the officers
and crew, for the part I had acted; and their best
wishes for my future prosperity and success.

As soon as I got on shore, I went to a printer, and
had a hand-bill struck off; which was afterwards of great
use to me. I then went home, but did not venture
abroad, as I was fearful of being apprehended, and
could not tell what troubles I might fall into. About
three weeks after my return, the Right Hon. Lord
R——, and his lady, came to Beer, for the purpose of
visiting a charity school, of which they were the bene-
factors. When we heard of their arrival, my wife
followed them, and presented one of my hand-bills to
his lordship, begging that he would be pleased to read
it; this he did with considerable attention, and as he
went down the street, he said, that he would do something for me. In about an hour after, he returned;
he said to some one near him, " Where is the good

woman who was speaking to me about her husband?"
My wife then advanced, and when his lordship saw her,
he said, "I am sorry that I cannot do any thing for
your husband, as I am informed that he was the man
who threatened to cut my sergeant's guts out." When
I heard this, knowing her ladyship was gone out of the
village, I ran after her, and as soon as I had overtaken
her carriage, I fell down on my knees, and presented
one of my hand-bills, entreating her ladyship to use
her influence with his lordship in my behalf, and that
the sergeant might not be allowed to take me. She then
said, "You ought to go back on board a man-of-war, and
be equal to Lord Nelson, you have such spirits for
fighting. If you do so, you may depend I will take care
that you shall not be hurt." I replied, "My lady, I
have ever had an aversion to the navy; I wish to remain
with my wife and family, and to support them in a
creditable manner, and therefore can never think of
returning." Her ladyship then said, "I will consider
about it," and turned off. About a week afterwards,
the soldiers were ordered away from Beer, as I con-
jecture, through the influence of her ladyship, and the
humanity of Lord R——.

CHAPTER V.

I now felt a great weight removed from my mind. I was freed from the fears that had so long haunted my walks by day, and my pillow by night, and I would gladly have entered on a new course of life ; but I found myself entangled with difficulties, from which I was unable to escape, and bound by a chain of circumstances whose links I was unable to break.

Accordingly I went to Alderney, and took in a cargo, but returning home, we were overtaken by foul weather, and in a gale of wind we lost our mast, about three leagues off from land ; we saved our rigging, however, by means of a tackle, and gave thirty guineas to the master of a Brixham fishing boat, with which we fell in, to tow us into that port. This was in the month of January, 1809. In July following, I went to Dartmouth, and bought a vessel, called the Lively ; which we afterwards sold to pay for the repairs of the other.

I now seriously resolved to abandon the trade of smuggling ; to take a public house, and to employ my leisure hours in fishing, &c. At first the house appeared to answer pretty well, but after being in it for two years, I found that I was considerably gone back in the world ; and that my circumstances, instead of

improving, were daily getting worse, for all the money
I could get by fishing and piloting, went to the brewer,
with whom the business was confined ; and the times
were very hard, trade and commerce being in a state
of great stagnation, and little or no prospect of their
revival.   Thus situated, and not knowing what else to
do, I now returned to my old trade of smuggling, and
in November 1812, went in a vessel to Alderney, but
returning home, about the middle of the channel, at
day-break, we fell in with one of his majesty's cruisers,
which afterwards proved to be the Catherine brig,
commanded by Captain Tipgle.   A very warm chase
then ensued, in the course of which, she fired twenty-
four cannon-shot at us ; in consequence of which we
were thrown into the greatest alarm, not knowing
whether we had fallen in with a French privateer, or an
English vessel.   About half-past ten o'clock in the
morning they came so near to us, that finding that
there was no hope of escaping, we hauled down all
our sails.   The crew, however, still kept up an incessant fire of small arms upon us, several of which
went through our binnacle and bulwarks, and the sails
we had hauled down.   All the men except myself were
below, and in the midst of this tremendous volley, I
escaped without a single wound ; a circumstance on
which I have since reflected, not without wonder; but
my mind was then in such a state of excitement, that
I thought but little of the danger to which I was exposed.

When the captain came within hail of us, he called
out, " You rascals, I will put you all on board a man-
of-war."   To his great disappointment, however, upon

inspecting our vessel, he found nothing on board her, except a pint of gin in a bottle; but he detained the vessel; and, having put myself and my companions on board his own brig, took us into Brixham. The same day, I asked the captain to grant me leave to go on shore, which he peremptorily refused; and when he went off in a boat himself, he gave the men a very particular charge to take care of us. Still I was not disheartened, and on his return to the brig, I determined to make another application; accordingly I went below to him, and renewed my request, but I met with another denial. I then said to him, " You have behaved towards me most shamefully : you have taken my vessel on the high seas, and detained it, though you found nothing on board to justify you in doing so; and it is, I conceive, an act of piracy." To this he replied, " I care nothing about it; you have given me a great deal of trouble, and I will not let you go on shore, unless I receive orders to that effect from the board." The following day, the Catherine brig being convoy to the Brixham fishermen, he went to sea, and took us cruising with him for about a week. When we came into the bay again, I once more reiterated my request, but with no better success; and, as he stepped over the side of the vessel to go on shore, he told the crew to keep a sharp look-out, for if they suffered one of us to escape, one of them should suffer in his stead. The same day, my wife, having heard of my situation, with some other females, the wives of my companions, came on board. Our interview was short; but long enough for me to entreat her to get a good boat, and to come

off to me the next morning. In the evening, I opened
part of my plan to my companions; and desired them
to be prepared to act according to the hints I had given
them. When she came, which was about ten o'clock
in the morning, the other officers being on shore, the
second mate had the charge of the vessel, which was
a circumstance favourable to my design. As soon as
she and the other females were alongside, I jumped
into the boat, and made a motion to my companions
to do the same, that we might assist them on board;
one of them did so, and I whispered to him to wait till
they were all out of the boat; and, immediately upon
this being accomplished, I called out aloud, "Shove
off!" upon which, three other of my companions jumped
in. I then put my oar against the side of the vessel;
but the second mate caught hold of it, and broke off the
blade. Being very angry, I threw the remaining part
at him, and called to my companions to hoist the sail.
He exclaimed, "If you do, I'll fire at you;" to which
I replied, "Make sure of your mark." At this he fired,
and the shot went through the sails; he was preparing
to do so again, when my wife wrested the piece out of
his hands. Having recovered it, he fired again, and the
shot striking the rope of the sail, it fell down. He then
stopped firing, thinking that we were sufficiently terrified to induce us to return to the ship. But in the
mean time, we had hoisted our sail up again, and pushed
off. They then got the boat out, and chased us, keeping up a continual fire at us; but, though the sails
were full of shot-holes, none of the men received any
injury. We put in at a promontory called Bob's Nose;

my companions jumped out : I was the last man, having steered the boat ; and as I was in the act of doing so, a shot passed close to my head, but did not touch me.

As soon as I got on shore, I scrambled up the cliffs ; and, when I had reached the top, I looked back, but could see no one. I then took off my jacket, and left it behind me, thinking that if they met with it, they would suppose that I had thrown it off to facilitate my speed in getting away. After this, I rolled myself down the cliffs, not far from where we landed. At the same time, I saw our pursuers following my companions, and several hundred people on Brixham hills, looking on ; but they were too far off to give them the least assistance. It was now about eleven o'clock ; I was without hat or jacket, and the rain descended in torrents. I found out the best retreat I could among the rocks, and remained there till four o'clock in the afternoon. About one, I saw the men belonging to the brig go by and embark ; and, when all seemed quiet, I started over hedges, fields, and ditches, and got to Torquay ; and went to a public-house kept by a friend, where I got dry clothes and refreshments. I then sent a man and horse to my wife, and directed her to meet me on the next day. The following morning I received a letter, informing me that two of my companions were retaken ; and, when my wife arrived, she told me that they had both been sentenced to go on board a man-of-war, bound for the West Indies. We then set off together, and got home safe to Beer.

CHAPTER VI.

WE remained in the public-house until November, 1813; when, in consequence of bad debts, several misfortunes, and the general stagnation of trade at that period, we shut it up, being unable to carry it on any longer. My situation was now a very deplorable one, for I had a wife and four children to support; my money was all gone, there was scarcely any thing to be done in smuggling, and I had nothing left but a boat, in which myself and my eldest son were accustomed to go fishing, that being the employment in which we were engaged during the summer, and in which we met with very indifferent success.

In the fall of the same year, another calamity overtook us, which for a time destroyed all my hopes; for, while following the occupation I have described, a gale of wind came on, which made us scud towards the shore; but, before we could reach it, a very heavy sea broke over the boat, which shattered her to pieces, so that it was with difficulty that we escaped with our lives. I had now lost my all, and the winter was coming on, which made us very disconsolate; but it passed away better than we could expect, for two vessels were driven into the bay by stress of weather,

which I was engaged in piloting; and, as they paid
me very handsomely, my domestic troubles were not
only lightened by this means, but I was likewise enabled
to pay ten pounds to the spirit merchant, with whom
I was in arrears when I left the public-house.

In January, 1814, being on the cliffs near Beer, on
the look-out, I spied a vessel about two leagues off to
the southward; and perceived, by means of my glass,
that she was a Dutch galliot, and in danger of becoming
a wreck. On seeing this, I immediately procured a
boat and men, and went off to her assistance; but a
custom-house boat, which was on the look-out, saw
me, and got to the vessel first. When I was on board,
I found, that in order to make sure of the job, they
were offering to take her into port for thirty pounds.
Upon this, I told the captain that they knew but little
about pilotage, and had no right to undertake it. He
then said that he would employ me, and have nothing
to do with them. When they heard this, the custom-
house men proposed for me to do it, and that I should
allow them their share of the thirty pounds. The captain
then asked what I would do it for, and whether I would
agree to the proposition which they had made. To
which I replied, that I would give them their share of
the sum they had proposed, or settle the matter by
arbitration afterwards; but that I would not undertake
to put the vessel into Brixham, which was the port he
wished to go to, for less than one hundred pounds.
These terms were mutually agreed to; and, having
rigged a jury mast, I piloted the vessel safe into Brixham the same afternoon. In the evening, I waited on

. the agent, and he told me to call on him the next day, and he would pay me the money, according to the agreement. As soon as I had received it, I satisfied the men I had employed, for the assistance they had rendered me, and gave the custom-officers their proportion of the sum which they had fixed on. With this, however, they were not contented, but put in a claim to a full share of the hundred pounds; and, as I refused to comply with their extortionate and unjust demand, they summoned me to appear before the magistrates. There a minute investigation took place; and, after I had been put to my oath on the point, they acknowledged that it was according to their agreement; and then, being asked how they could expect any more, they had nothing to say for themselves, upon which the magistrates dismissed the case, and sent them about their business. In consequence of this, they were continually annoying me, by overhauling my bags and other things, in the expectation of finding smuggled articles, and with a view of injuring myself and family; but, a short time after, the sitter of the boat, who was my greatest enemy, was taken off in a very sudden and awful manner, for as he was riding along the road near Seaton, he fell from his horse, and pitching forward on his face into a small stream of water about four inches deep, he was drowned.

About this time, the beginning of the year 1814, trade being extremely dull, in consequence of the fluctuating nature of our public affairs, smuggling was also at a stand. Being, however, always on the look-out, through having a large family, I heard that

Mr. Down, a gentleman then residing at Bridport, wanted a person to rig a vessel, and go fishing for him. Immediately upon receiving this intelligence, I went to him, and offered to undertake the job ; and, finding from inquiries, that I was capable of doing it, he agreed to employ myself and son on very liberal terms. We then went to Bridport, and were engaged in this work from the month of February till the latter end of April, when the vessel was ready for sea. Mr. Down then paid myself and my son at the rate of twenty-seven shillings per week for our joint labour, and likewise discharged our bill at the public-house for board and lodging during the whole time we were employed about it. We then went fishing in the vessel till July, and were paid by the share. We found, however, that this speculation would not answer, Bridport being an inconvenient place to go in and out at. Our employer then ordered the vessel to be laid up, and we went home again. This engagement proved a great relief to my circumstances, every kind of trade being, as I before observed, very dead.

CHAPTER VII.

In the month of August in the same year, out of
the money which I received of Mr. Down, I bought
another boat, in which I went fishing for a few times;
but, as Cherburg was open for smuggling, I took my
son and two men went me, and went thither for that
purpose. Our first voyage took a fortnight in com-
pleting: we landed, however, all safe, and it turned
out a very profitable one, which set me up in the world
again, and revived all my ardour for speculation. The
second, having some business to transact, I staid at
home: it was performed in ten days, and proved likewise successful. The third also, I remained on shore,
and sent a man in my place; on their return, the men
sunk the goods, and on landing, the tide-waiter seized
the boat, which we lost, but saved the cargo.

In September I went in a boat belonging to another
man, with three other persons, to Cherburg; on our
return we sunk the goods, and finally landed all safe.
In November, I again proceeded to the same place, and
we took in a cargo; but going back, in company with
two other smuggling boats, we were overtaken by a
most tremendous gale, which obliged us to sink our
goods, and run ashore. The next day, the officers

seized the boats; and on the following morning, the
custom-house boat ran over our buoy, and they took
up all the kegs, amounting to upwards of one hundred.
This was a severe loss. In the latter end of September
I went to Cherburg with two other men, where by
appointment, we met a Frenchman, who lent us his
vessel, for which we agreed to give him twenty-five
pounds for one voyage. Having loaded her, we put to
sea, but a gale of wind coming on, we were detained
in the channel three days, and the vessel being very
leaky, we sunk our goods, and put into Lyme Cob; a
few days after the weather became calm; we then went
for our goods, and got them on shore, without meeting
with any interruption. In January 1815, I went again
to Cherburg, with another man, in a vessel which we
hired; our voyage was a very troublesome one, and
lasted fourteen days; on our return, when we arrived
at an open beach, we were on the point of landing,
when we were put off, by a signal from our friends;
some revenue officers and soldiers being on the look-
out. We then sunk our goods, but not being able to
get any opportunity of taking them up again for nearly
three weeks, during which time the weather was very
frosty, the spirits became thick, and so much injured
in quality, that we were obliged to sell them for what
we could get; after which I remained on shore till
March, when I bought half a boat, and again proceeded
on a voyage to Cherburg, with two other men; we
made a good voyage in six days, and landed safe and
well. We then set out on another trip; but having
engaged to send six kegs of spirits to Lyme, as the

men, three in number, were carrying them, they were seized by the custom-house officers, who afterwards came to an agreement with the men, to take them to their house; but in consequence of one of the men running away with some of the kegs, they detained the other two in custody, and they were to be brought to trial. I being absent at the time, my wife got bail for their appearance. When I came home, about a fortnight after, I went to the trial, and the men were fined twenty-five pounds each, besides expences, which I and my partners paid for them, it being one concern. This was a very great loss, and severely felt by me. I made several other voyages to Cherburg this summer, all of which were attended with success, except one, when we lost half the cargo.

In the month of October, in the same year, I went with another man to Exmouth, where we bought a vessel, called the Volante, for which we gave two hundred pounds; we then took her into Lyme, to have her bowsprit stemmed, after which we went smuggling in her, and though she was very leaky, we continued to make good voyages in her, all the winter. We then laid her up, to have her timbers fastened, and to undergo a general repair. About this time, a circumstance occurred, which though trivial in itself, occasioned me a great deal of vexation and trouble. It happened that a smuggling boat was taken, with one man in her, about half a league from Beer, by the Vigilant cutter; and being acquainted with him, I went on board that vessel, with his brother and four others, to see if we could render him any assistance. The

captain being a good-natured man, I ventured to ask
him to let the smuggler, who was his prisoner, go
ashore with us. This he refused, saying, that it was
not in his power; but at parting, he gave us a bottle
of gin. This I had in my possession, and when we
landed on the beach, a tide-waiter, who was then
measuring culm, asked me what I had got. I replied,
"A drop of gin." He then collared me, and insisted upon
having it, but being determined to disappoint him, I
threw it into the sea. He then wrote against me to the
board, stating that I had obstructed him in the
performance of his duty. A short time afterwards, an
order came from the board for my apprehension, and
he came to my house, attended by some soldiers, to
take me up. I immediately surrendered myself, and
they took me before the magistrates, who bound me
over to appear at the ensuing Lammas Assizes, 1815, at
Exeter, and ordered me to find bail in the sum of two
hundred pounds. When the time arrived, I went, and
employed Attorney Kingdon and Counsellor Moore to
conduct my defence. The cause was brought into
court; and the judge, after hearing the evidence, con-
sidered it frivolous and vexatious, and I was honourably
acquitted.

CHAPTER VIII.

OUR vessel the Volante, being repaired and ready for sea, we made a few good voyages in her; but on our return from the last, having left the vessel lying in Lyme Cob, a violent storm came on, and the tide flowing to a great and unusual height, she ran ashore, and with several others, was dashed to pieces; we succeeded however, though with considerable difficulty, in saving the materials.

The following year, in February 1816, a fishing sloop, called the Elizabeth and Kitty, belonging to Brixham, was driven into Beer roads, in a gale of wind. When she came to an anchor, the crew left the vessel, and took to the boat, in which they reached the shore, at the imminent peril of their lives. Having an excellent row-boat, with my son and two others, I went off to her, and when I came on board, I found her water-logged, the water being up to the cabin lockers. At first it was my intention to have carried her into Lyme, but the wind blowing hard, and having no pump-gear, I was fearful that she would not reach that port, I therefore run her ashore on Seaton beach. For the preservation of the vessel, I received salvage as a remuneration. I afterwards agreed to purchase this

sloop of the owners, and having come to terms, I got
her off, and took her into Axmouth harbour to be
repaired, and then let her out for fishing, &c. This
summer, I was seized with a violent fit of sickness, by
which my strength was so much impaired, that I made
but two voyages during the course of it.   In September
I went passenger in my own sloop the Elizabeth and
Kitty, to Cherburg, where I hired a French vessel
to bring home the cargo, with which I arrived safe, and
made a good voyage. I then sent the French vessel
back.   In October, I divided my sloop into shares, and
with my partners, I made seven voyages in her.   The
first we did very well ; the second we got home safe,
having sunk the kegs; but through the roughness
of the weather, they broke loose, and drifted, and the
officers took the greatest part of them; the third was
a short voyage, and all well; the fourth I did not go
myself, having some business to transact at home, but
it turned out well ; the fifth we saved nearly the whole
cargo; the sixth proved a pretty good voyage; and
the seventh and last the best of all, for we landed all
our goods, and disposed of them advantageously.   We
then laid up the vessel.

CHAPTER IX.

In April 1817, I crossed to Cherburg in an open boat, with three other men, and made two safe voyages in succession. In July of the same year, I went in our vessel the Elizabeth and Kitty to Southampton, with a cargo of stones and coal, and having discharged it, we took in a load of slate, with which she went to sea, but having some business of importance to transact, I staid behind; but as soon as it was finished, I set off by coach; and on my return home, had the satisfaction to find that she was also arrived, and had discharged her cargo.

In October, one of my partners and myself went as passengers to Cherburg, where we hired a French vessel, and took in a cargo of contraband goods, with which we returned all well. We then made several other voyages there and back, sometimes safe, and others partly so. In the mean time the Elizabeth and Kitty was captured by the Vigilant cutter, and all her goods and one man taken, who being promised his liberty and twenty pounds, turned informer, and disclosed all particulars as to whom the goods belonged, &c. The vessel was then taken into Dartmouth, and forfeited to the government. In conjunction with two

others, I then bought a small French vessel, in which
we made several voyages, all safe and well, and carried
on a prosperous trade till the close of the year, which
in some degree, repaired the loss we had sustained.

In January 1817, a vessel that had been to Sidmouth
with coal, in a violent storm was driven into Loden bay,
where she was obliged to let go her anchor : she then
cut away her cable, and ran on shore at Seaton beach.
Being a fine vessel, and well adapted for coasting, a
friend and myself purchased her of Mr. Flinn, the
owner ; but she was so much damaged, that it was with
considerable difficulty that we succeeded in getting
her into Axmouth harbour. There we had her properly
repaired ; and in June she was ready for sea, when my
partner, together with my son, took the first voyage in
her, to Newkey, after a cargo of slate. In the mean
time, in connexion with some other smugglers, I had
a long open boat built in France; when she was finished,
which was in the month of July, I went over to
Cherburg, and having taken in a cargo of goods, and
employed Frenchmen to assist me in bringing her
home, we put to sea, but had not left the shore more
than two hours, when two long-boats belonging to the
custom-house gave chase to us; we then altered our
course, and succeeded in getting back again.

On the following morning, which was Wednesday,
we sailed again, but about four o'clock in the afternoon
another long-boat came alongside of us before we
perceived her. She chased us for about three hours,
and then boarded us, but found nothing, we having
thrown our kegs out ; we were, however, taken into

E

Alderney, and put on board the Adder. The captain then examined us, but finding that it was a French boat manned with French sailors, and that I was rated a passenger, he told us to go about our business, adding, at the same time, " I have a great mind to keep you in consequence of your having given me so much trouble; and be sure, if ever I come across you again, to throw out your tubs fairly, that I may take them up;" to which proposition I agreed, being desirous of not throwing any obstacles in the way of regaining my liberty. After this, on Friday about twelve o'clock, we sailed from Alderney, and about half-past three we got to Cherburg, where we remained that night. On Saturday morning we took in another lot of goods; on Sunday we set sail, and arrived home on Monday; we then sunk our goods, and the Frenchmen put me on shore at Lyme, and took the long-boat back to France, but we had a great deal of difficulty in taking up our kegs, and lost a considerable part of them.

CHAPTER X.

By this time our vessel was arrived from Newkey with a cargo of slate : she then took in a load of culm, with which she proceeded to Charmouth, where she landed, but the crew were prevented from getting to sea again by a hard gale of wind ; and though she had an anchor out, the cable parting, she drifted ashore, and went to pieces. I then received a letter from my partner and son, giving an account of the misfortunes which had taken place, and desiring me to come to them with all speed ; I accordingly took a horse, and went to them as fast as possible. We succeeded in saving the sails and the greatest part of the materials, and carried them to Lyme, where they were deposited in a sail loft. When they had been put in order, and an estimate taken of them, I bought my partner's half, for which I gave him the trifling sum of thirteen pounds. This was a very great loss to us both, for the vessel had cost two hundred pounds, and she had only made her second voyage.

In August, a French vessel in which I had a share came to Lyme, and together with another smuggler I went over to Cherburg in her, and the speculation turned out profitable. One of my creditors at. this time (the brewer to whom I was in debt one hundred pounds when I declined keeping the public house) having heard that I had purchased the wreck at Lyme, took out a writ against me: upon this I went to his house, and agreed to give him twenty-five pounds in hand and twenty-five pounds afterwards; and having paid these sums he gave me a full discharge, so that I was once more clear of the world, which was a great satisfaction to my mind.

I then went smuggling again, and made several voyages, some of which were productive of gain, and others proved unsuccessful. In the latter part of the year, the wind blowing very strong, a Swedish schooner drove into the bay; being on the look-out I saw her, and immediately went on board and agreed with the captain to take him into Lyme for forty pounds; but the vessel was in such a leaky state, that I was obliged with their assistance to use every exertion to save her. At last, however, we accomplished our design, and got her in safe, at which the captain was so much pleased, that he paid the money without the least grudging.

In January, 1818, I was laid up by a severe fit of the gout, which continued two months; this proved a considerable hinderance to me in business, and threw me greatly back in the world, for I had a large family. When I recovered from my illness and got about again, I employed my time for the remainder of the year, and the spring of the next, in fishing and smuggling, in which I was pretty successful.

In June, 1819, together with another smuggler I

went to Cherburg, and having taken in a cargo, we
put to sea in the long-boat of which I have before
spoken. When off Start Point we fell in with the Sea-
gull, a tender belonging to the Adder sloop of war.
The sea being very calm, we perceived her when she
was a great way off, and got alongside of a large
Dutch ship, in the hopes of being thereby concealed
from the observation of the enemy ; there we remained
for some time, but at last the crew on board the tender
spied us, upon which they hove out their boat and
gave chase. We then spread all the canvas we could,
and tried to make our escape; but having no wind,
and four Frenchmen on board, who were indifferent
sailors, and theirs being a fine boat, and well manned,
they at last came up with us, but they could not
find a single article on board to confirm the suspicion
of our being smugglers, nor had they seen us throw
any thing out. While they were deliberating how to
act, the sitter of the boat recollected my physiognomy,
and that I had promised the captain before when I
was taken, that if they fell in with me again, I would
throw my kegs over fairly, that he might pick them up,
on which condition he had engaged that I should not
be injured. He then took me on board the tender;
and as soon as the commander saw me, he exclaimed,
" Are not you a pretty fellow to throw your things
out in such a manner after promising so fair, and
the lenity I showed towards you?" He then said,
that there was a new act respecting smugglers, and
that he should take us into Dartmouth. When we
arrived there, he took us to the custom-house to be

examined by the collector, and he not being come to the office, I seized an opportunity, and made my escape in a small boat across the water to King's Wear, and from thence to Brixham.

The same afternoon I received a letter from a landlord at Dartmouth, informing me that the case had been investigated at the custom-house, and nothing found against me; and requesting that I would come over about the Frenchmen's bill. Accordingly I went to his house on the following Sunday, but had scarcely sat down, when I was surrounded by the men belonging to the tender by whom I was first taken, who insisted on my going with them as their prisoner. Being greatly aggravated by this piece of treachery, I told them that I would not, and prepared to make all the resistance in my power. They then sent a man away, who returned with two constables; and upon hearing the case, they said, that as it was Sunday, they had no business with me without a warrant from the magistrates, and would not interfere. The men belonging to the tender finding I was resolute, asked me if I would give them my passport, and appear on the morrow: to this I agreed; they then departed, and I returned home. About three weeks after an order came down from the board, for the boat to be delivered up: we then sent her back to France, and I and my companions once more got safe out of the difficulty in which we had been involved.

CHAPTER XI.

Soon after this business was settled, I and one of my companions went as passengers in a boat to France. Off Portland, we again fell in with the boat belonging to the same cutter; but, having a complaint in my eyes, my face was so muffled up that the sitter did not know me, and asked my companions what was the matter with that old fellow; to which they made some indifferent answer. The cutter was by this time come up within hail, and the commander ordered his people to bring the person who had the command of the boat on board, which they did. He then examined him, and asked several questions, and amongst others, what was become of me; and said, "Tell Rattenbury, when you see him, that if ever I fall in with him again, I will hang him up at the yard-arm, because he destroys all." He then sent the captain of our boat about his business; and the circumstance of their not recollecting me, afforded no small merriment to us all. Having got rid of the cutter, we proceeded on our voyage to Cherburg, where we hired a vessel, and staid two or three days taking in our cargo; after which we put to sea again, and got home safe and all well. In September, the same year, my partner went to Dartmouth, and re-purchased the Elizabeth and Kitty, the vessel we had lost; and in October he got her ready for sea, and we made a voyage in her to Cherburg, where we took in a cargo of goods, which we brought home and landed all safe.

Our second voyage, which was to the same place, likewise proved successful; but the third, between Lyme and Seaton, when about a league off from shore, we spied a sail; and, being suspicious, we then hauled our wind, and went about to the eastward, but we being in the moon of the vessel, they could see our motions, though we could not see theirs. We then kept away to the westward; and, about half an hour after, we perceived that it was a cutter in pursuit of us. Soon after, she came up, and fired several musket shots at us; we then hauled our boat up, and I told the people to get into her as quick as possible, and hold her on till I was ready. I then laid down the helm, and jumped in; and, while the cutter was luffing to avoid running on board our vessel, we made our escape, leaving behind us three hundred kegs of spirits, besides several bales of tea. We then spread all the sail we could, and got on shore about a mile and a half from Beer, being afraid to land there, lest the crew of the cutter might be in pursuit of us. We then made the best of our way home, leaving our boat behind. A few days after, I heard that the captain was at Lyme: I sent my wife to him, to request that he would be so kind as to deliver up the clothes belonging to the people, as they had left all on board; and he told her, if I would come for them, I should have them.

I then went to him, and he received me very civilly, being, as I suppose, in a good temper at having taken so fine a prize. In the course of our interview, he showed me a pocket-book which he had found, and asked me if it was mine. I replied, it was not, but that I knew who it belonged to; and if he would have the goodness to entrust it to me, I would deliver it to the owner. He then gave me the pocket-book, and all the clothes; and I returned home, depressed in spirits at the loss I had sustained, but endeavouring to console myself with the thought that it might have been worse, for I was still in the possession of liberty. This happened in November, 1819.

In the latter end of December, I went again over to Cherburg, in a vessel as passenger with another man; and, having taken in our cargo, we set sail on the 2nd of January, 1820, and the next morning arrived off the English coast, and the sea being calm, we took our goods in the boat with the intention of landing them; but we had not left the vessel more than three quarters of an hour, when a tremendous gale of wind came on, accompanied with heavy snow showers, which half filled the boat, and the air was so intensely cold, that we were almost frozen. We remained in this situation till the next morning, not being able to see the vessel through the density of the atmosphere, nor the people on board her to see us. About seven o'clock, having spied the signal we had hoisted, they came alongside, and took us on board, where we shifted our clothes, all hands being half dead with the sufferings we had endured; and, having sunk our kegs, we went on shore.

Some of these, however, afterwards drifted through the violence of the gale, and were lost.

About the same time, the little French vessel, of which I had purchased half, came out of Cherburg; and fell in with the Hind sloop of war, and was captured, with all her cargo. This, as may be imagined, threw a fresh gloom over my spirits, and was a great crush to all my hopes; but when the mind has been long trained in the school of adversity, it becomes callous to disappointments; and though its ardour may be a while repressed, its powers of endurance are not easily subdued.

CHAPTER XII.

In the month of February, 1820, I went with three other passengers to Cherburg, where we hired a French vessel; and, having taken in our cargo, got home with the loss of part of it. We then sent the vessel back. About this period, I was laid up with a severe attack of the gout, which lasted six weeks. When the disorder relaxed its grasp, and I was able to walk about again, being on the beach at Beer, in the month of May, I accidentally met with a gentleman just as he landed; and, falling into conversation with him, found that he was come into the neighbourhood for the purpose of making aquatic excursions during the summer; and, having ascertained this point, I made him a tender of my services. Not being able to find a vessel to his mind, he bought a boat which I then had, and converted it into a pleasure yacht, and employed my son constantly, and myself occasionally, when he went to sea. I accompanied him to Sidmouth, Dartmouth, Brixham, and other places on the western coast; and afterwards, as the summer advanced, to Guernsey and Jersey with a party of his friends. At the latter place I was taken extremely ill, and I can never forget the kindness and humanity with which he provided medical

assistance for me, and supplied my various wants till
I recovered. We then resumed our expedition; and,
after having seen whatever was remarkable in the
channel islands, returned back, and arrived at Seaton,
where we put the ladies and gentlemen on shore; who
were all much delighted with the tour they had made,
and the many curious objects and interesting scenes
they had examined in the course of it, while I felt no
less grateful for the kindness which they had shown
towards me, and the liberal manner in which they
promised to reward my services and attendance; but in
this I was sadly disappointed.

This summer I bought a small spot of ground with
the view of building a house, and went with my boat
along the cliffs, picking up stones to erect it with. I
then busily employed myself in getting all the materials
ready for the carpenters and masons to begin their
work; and in this manner I was engaged till the fall
of the year.

In September I went to sea with some friends to
take up some kegs which we had sunk; and it being
night, a preventive boat came close up to us before
we saw her. One of the men then laid hold of the out-
rigger, but by a sudden jerk I shook his hand off from
it, and put our boat out of their grasp. Having no
sail, they were obliged to take to their oars; they then
chased and fired at us, but a fine breeze springing up,
the longer they pursued the more we left them astern.
Finding their efforts useless, they gave up the chace,
and we got safe on shore.

During the remainder of the fair weather this year,

I was employed in assisting about my house, and in attending the gentleman I have before mentioned; whenever he went to sea, or required my services. In the month of November I had a boat which came home, and having sunk her goods was driven on shore; and just after this misfortune took place, another boat which belongèd to me was stranded on Stapen sands, where she was dashed to pieces, and the greater part of the goods became the prey of the inhabitants. In the same month I went to Weymouth, and took all the money I could collect, and paid to my merchants. While I was there, the Lyme packet, bound for Guernsey, with passengers, drove in, in consequence of a gale of wind; and the captain getting drunk on Saturday, which was the day on which he had appointed to sail, all the passengers left him. On Sunday he put to sea, and myself and one of my partners went with him to Cherburg, where we took a cargo on board, with which we returned as passengers in the same vessel. When we came under Salcombe hill, which was in about fourteen hours, we hove the boat out, and a boy that was with us and myself went into her to try to get on shore, but the surf was so great near the beach, that we found it impossible to land; and on going off again with the intention of returning to the vessel, we could not find her through the haziness of the weather. We then made another attempt at landing; the first sea we saved, but seeing there was great danger from the second, I jumped overboard, and swam to the shore; and upon looking round, had the satisfaction to find that the boy also had escaped, but the boat had capsized. We then went forward to Sidmouth as fast as possible, where we found some of the men belonging to the packet who had come on shore, and I sent them after the boat. The next morning, about the dawn of the day, we saw the packet about a mile off from land, and I was informed she had sunk about one hundred and twenty kegs. Soon after this the captain and the crew became intoxicated, in consequence of which they ran alongside the Scourge cutter, and were taken. When the capture took place, some of the men were in the act of throwing the remaining part of the cargo overboard; one lot of the kegs was picked up by the people belonging to the Scourge floating on the waves, and when they came on board the packet, they found the captain and two of the sailors quite drunk. The crew then being promised a reward, turned informers; the first lot of goods consisted of about six-score kegs, which the Scourge took up, and proceeded with them to Exmouth. When they got over the bar, my partner and the master of the packet gave information respecting the rest of the cargo, which the cutter likewise took up, and the captain of the Scourge then gave the money which he had promised to my partner and the master of the packet, which they shared between them. They were afterwards taken before the magistrates at Exeter, and my partner, being a passenger, was set free; but the captain and one of his men were sent to jail. After doing me all the injury they could, in the manner I have described, they then swore that the goods belonged to me, and that I was the sole proprietor of them, though I was only a passenger, (the same as

my partner, who was cleared,) and on shore at the time
when the vessel and cargo were taken. Of all these
particulars I was afterwards informed, but the information did not reach me till it was too late to be of
any particular benefit to me, as will be seen in the
sequel. About a fortnight after this melancholy ca-
tastrophe I went to sea in a large·open boat, with
another man and two of my sons. Off Salterton we
fell in with the Scourge cutter, and not knowing what
had been said of me, but being suspicious that all had
not been right, I used my utmost endeavours to get
away from her; but as she perceived us, she gave
chace, and fired upon the whole eighteen cannon-shots
at us.

When we got on shore we found several men from
the cutter had arrived there before, and were waiting
for us ; they said that the captain had given them
orders to detain my boat, to which I replied they should
not; and I immediately took up a large stone and
hove it into the boat, with an intention to stave her;
but in consequence of their superior numbers, and
being armed with authority, they at last, however,
accomplished their point, and having taken the boat
they towed her into Tospham, where she was laid up
in the mud. By this means I was kept out of employ
till the end of December, having no other boat to go
to sea in, which was a great injury to myself and
family, particularly at this period; as my circumstances,
through the numerous and heavy losses which I had
met with, were now in a very declining state.

CHAPTER XIII.

On the 1st of January, 1821, being then entering the forty-third year of my age, I went on board a French vessel with three others as passengers to Cherburg, where we arrived the next day; we then took in our cargo. On the 4th we sailed, and on the 5th we arrived home with our goods, with which we did very well, *all safe*. On the 6th I went to Torquay and joined our vessel; and on the following day, the 7th, we put to sea with the wind to the eastward. About a league from Portland, the next day we fell in with the Greyhound cutter, with a smuggling vessel which she had just captured. The commander then sent a boat alongside our vessel to take our captain on board the cutter, where he was examined and dismissed, they not being able to find any thing against him. About twelve o'clock the same day, the 8th, we saw a brig with her colours up, as a signal of distress. We therefore bore down to her, and when we came alongside found she was a Swedish vessel laden with salt, that had drifted from her anchor, and was in want of provisions and a pilot. Having parted with such articles of food as we could spare, I went on board and offered my services to the captain, who told me that he wanted

to go to Cowes; that, I told him, was impossible, as
the wind was south-east; but if he wished it, I would
undertake to put her into Weymouth or Dawlish.
After a little consideration he decided in favour of the
former place, as that was the nearest port, and he
agreed to give me eighty pounds for my assistance.
We then made all the sail we could, and in three hours
and a half we were in Weymouth roads. There
another pilot came on board with the agent, and having
left a young man that was with me behind, I returned
to our vessel, and we proceeded on our voyage.
The next morning about day-break, we fell in with an
Indiaman that supplied us with such articles of provisions as we were in need of, but he did not want
any assistance. On the following day, the 11th, we
arrived at Cherburg, and having taken in our cargo,
sailed on the 13th, and got home with our goods, part
of which we afterwards lost, but saved some and did
pretty well.

CHAPTER XIV.

On the 29th of January, we went again as passengers to France, and on our return, having a cargo of goods, consisting of one hundred kegs of spirits, and a bale of tea, as we were working down with another smuggling vessel which was bound to Exmouth harbour, about a league or more off Budleigh Salterton, we wound away, and then got our boat out and put all the goods into her, and veered the boat astern. About five minutes afterwards, we saw a boat, which we perceiving to be a king's boat, cut away our boat from the stern, upon which she came alongside of us, and the captain attempted to come on board, but we told him to keep off. They again attempted to board us, but we shoved her off with a boat-hook; upon which, she dropped astern of our vessel, and began to fire at us. The first shot carried away our main halliards, and down came the sails: she then rode up again under the stern, and then renewed the fire; upon which one of our men hove a shy-stone at the boat, which pitched on the gunnel instead of going into it. They still kept firing, and several shots went through the counter and companion of the vessel, and they continued to fire till their ammunition was quite

exhausted, upon which he rode up alongside the vessel,
and I asked him what he wanted; he recollected my
voice, and said, " Master Rattenbury, you had better
let me come alongside quietly." I then prevailed on
the crew, English and French, to do so. He then came
on board and searched the vessel, but found nothing.
I then asked him to take refreshments, which he did ;
he inquired about the other vessel, and I told him it
was a pilot sloop : but whilst they were with me, our
vessel ran alongside the boat which we had laden with
our goods, so that our crew were obliged to shove her
off with a boat-hook to prevent a discovery. Soon
afterwards, our crew became very mutinous ; and I have
every reason to believe, that dreadful consequences
would have ensued, had it not been for my interference.
Captain Stocker remained till three o'clock in the
morning, and having no plea for detaining the vessel,
he then left ; but when he had got about twenty yards
distance, he called out to me and said, " Mind, Mr.
Rattenbury, I do not find you here in the morning with
the vessel ; if you are, I'll detain you." A fine breeze
springing up from the N.N.W. we cruised about in
search of our boat, but could not find her. The next
morning at day-break, we saw Captain Stocker with
two Salterton boats a long way off, and they had our
boat in tow, containing the goods, with them. We
then made the best of our way to Beer, and returned
to France the same day, for fear of being apprehended ;
and remained there a fortnight, and then came home
with a cargo. I then went on shore, and sent a crew
off to the vessel to secure the goods ; but about ten

o'clock at night the wind was blowing very hard, E.N.E. and a tremendous sea hauled the stem of the boat out.

The next morning the crew came on shore, and gave an account of the accident they had met with; I then went cruising for the tubs, but a gale of wind coming on, I was obliged to run ashore at Sidmouth, and the best of the goods were driven on shore at Penton, near Torbay.

In the month of February, as I was on the cliffs on the look-out, I saw the mate of the Scourge; and having heard that he had been making inquiries after me the night before, I went up to him and asked if he wanted me, and he said, " Yes, I have a spyglass belonging to you; and if you will come on board the cutter, I will give it you." After a little more con-versation we parted. I then took my boat and my two little boys, and went on board; when I arrived, I was told that the mate was at breakfast with another person. I then sent my little boys below, and after waiting some time on deck, I went down also. When I had been on board about an hour, the mate sent for me, and when I went into his cabin, there was a de-putation officer and another man with him; the mate then took out a writ which had been issued against me in consequence of the information of Cowley, the captain of the packet, and having read it, the deputa-tion officer said that I was his prisoner. It is impossible for me to describe my feelings on finding I had been trepanned in such a manner; and when the deputation officer desired me to go below, I positively declared that

I would not; and when one of the men asked me what I was going to do with the boys, (the one five, and the other nine years of age at the time,) being goaded to madness by the question, I replied in a rage, "Throw them overboard if you like, and drown them, for you might as well do so, as to take their father from them in such a clandestine manner." I then asked the mate to let me go on shore and try to get bail; but as the fine was for so large a sum, viz. four thousand five hundred pounds, he told me it was not in his power.

The mate then sent my two little boys on shore, and when the boat returned, which was in less than half an hour, made all sail for Exmouth. About two o'clock we got to the foot of the bar: the mate then sent me below with the deputation officer and steward, till we arrived; he then came below himself, and said, "You may go on deck if you please." There I met the captain, who had just come on board, and on my addressing him on the subject of my arrest, he said, "I know nothing about it; I have nothing against you myself: it is all Cowley's concern." I was then taken on shore, where a coach was waiting, into which the mate, the deputation officer, and myself, entered, one of the men belonging to the cutter, well armed, being on the outside as a guard. When we came to Exeter, I was taken under a very strong escort, armed with pistols, so that it was impossible to make any effort at escape, to the sheriff's office, where I again proposed putting in bail, but was told it would not be worth while, as the writ would be out in two days, and then I should be obliged to find special bail. The same day I was removed to

St. Thomas's ward, where I found my situation less uncomfortable than I had expected. At the ensuing assizes, I employed Mr. Cox the attorney, and Mr. Tyrrell the barrister, to carry on a trial against government, the writ having been served on the high seas, for which I paid them the sum of sixty-eight pounds, but lost the trial. Being now in great distress, I was engaged as a servant to the insolvent debtors till the 9th of August, when through an act of grace passed by his gracious majesty George the Fourth, I once more obtained my liberty, and returned home, where I was joyfully received by my wife and family.

CHAPTER XV.

WHEN I got a little settled again, I engaged in smuggling, fishing, and piloting. On the 18th of December, 1825, as I was returning from a smuggling expedition, I was captured, off Dawlish, by the crew of a boat belonging to the coast-guard, and carried to Budleigh Salterton watch-house; where I remained until the 2nd of January, 1826, when an order arrived from the board for me to be taken before the magistrates, who committed me to Exeter jail.

Not being satisfied with the jail allowance, which consisted of twenty-two ounces of bread every morning, and ten pounds of potatoes and a pound of pork per week, I wrote a letter to the board for my pay instead; and, in consequence of it, on the 15th of February, received an order to be paid 4½d. per day.

One morning, when I had been in prison for about nine months, as the governor was in the hospital, one of the transports (with whom, together with persons who were in to take their trial for every description of crime, I was most unpleasantly associated,) gave him a blow on the head with a brush, which felled him senseless to the floor; upon which they all ran down into the day-room. The turnkeys directly gave the alarm, and myself and the other smugglers assisted in securing them before they had effected their escape. In consequence of this, the governor wrote a petition in our behalf to the board; but, unfortunately, it was of no benefit to us. About three months after this, I sent a letter to Sir William Pole, Bart.; who was so kind as to write a petition for me to the lords of the treasury, who sent word that, at the expiration of fifteen months from the period of my trial, I might be set at liberty. Accordingly, on the 5th of April, 1827, Mr. Hull, accompanied by the collector of the customs, called at the governor's house, and I signed a bond for five hundred pounds; when, through the goodness of God, and the influence of kind friends, I was once more free, and immediately returned home to my family at Beer.

CHAPTER XVI.

About the latter end of May, the Rev. Dr. Palmer, Major Still, and Major Pine, sent for me to attend them at Colyton, which I did; and found they wanted me to go to London, concerning the harbour which was then in contemplation at Beer, and the grand western canal, to extend from Beer to Thorverton, a distance of forty-two miles: to which proposal I readily consented. Dr. Palmer then gave me a guinea, and desired me to call at Mr. Sampson's at eight o'clock next morning, which I did; and the doctor took me in his gig to Shute House, where he alighted; and in about half an hour, Sir William came to the door, and said, "Here is Rob Roy come again;" and then ordered me into the house to take refreshments, and treated me very kindly. From thence, we proceeded to Chard, where I remained at an inn till the following morning; when Mr. Salter, the solicitor's clerk, called for me to go to London by the mail, where we arrived about eleven o'clock the next morning. On the ensuing day, I was desired to attend at the Western Canal Office; from which place, I went with some other persons to West-minster Hall, where I saw Lord Rolle, who ordered me to attend there every day till I was called, which was

F

not till the 14th of June. During all that time I
received one guinea per day, and had likewise all my
expences paid; so that I was extremely well pleased.
The counsellor who examined me in the House of
Commons, asked me what trade I followed : I told him
sometimes fishing, sometimes piloting, and sometimes
smuggling. Sir Isaac Coffin asked me several questions concerning the depth of the sea at various parts
of the bay from Portland to Start Point: how
I would get vessels round Portland in a gale of
wind S.S.W.; whether I had not seen a great many
vessels lost through not having a harbour; to which I
answered in the affirmative. My examination lasted,
in the whole, about three quarters of an hour; in the
course of which, I explained every thing relative to the
subject in the best manner I was able, and was told
that I conducted myself very well; and on the following morning, I went to the agent's office, and received
the money that was due to me ; and immediately took
a place in the coach, and returned to my family in
high spirits.

CHAPTER XVII.

I HAD been home about a fortnight, when I engaged in a smuggling expedition, which was accomplished in a week; and, on returning, we were chased by the Invincible cutter; but escaped in consequence of the night coming on. We sunk the kegs; but lost them through a man informing against us.

On the 2nd of July, the Right Hon. Lord Rolle sent for me to go to the House of Lords, concerning the canal and harbour. I immediately obeyed the summons; and arrived in London in the space of two days. The next morning, I went to Westminster Hall, where I saw Lord R. and Dr. Palmer; and was desired by them to be in attendance every day till I was called: which I promised to do. I then went to the Western Canal Office, where I received five pounds. On the third day, I was called to give evidence in the House of Lords; and, after the oath had been administered, I was examined and cross-examined, and explained every thing I was required to the best of my ability.

The next morning, Lord R. having desired me to call at his house in Grosvenor Square, I went, and he gave me half a guinea, and told me to go to the office for my money, which I did; and received twice as much as before, and returned home with blue ribbons in my hat, and a merry heart, from the expectation of deriving great advantage from the passing of the act;

but was sadly disappointed in the result, for notwithstanding the bill was passed, the project was entirely dropped.

I remained at home, engaged in my old occupations, until the year 1829, when I made an application to Lord R., who gave me a letter to the Admiral at Portsmouth. I went on board the Tartar cutter, and staid there two months before I went to the admiral's office, where I received an order to go on board the admiral's ship; but, not liking it, returned to the Tartar cutter, which was then at Cowes, where I remained on board as a seaman until November the 10th, when I was taken ill, and put on shore at Beer; and in the space of a week, the cutter came after me, and carried me to Weymouth, where I was placed in sick quarters ill the 6th of January, 1830. I then applied to Lieutenant Watson, who was on the point of leaving the Tartar, for my discharge, which he gave me. I then went to the custom-house for my pay, and went home, where I remained till March; when I went in a trader to London, to meet two of my sons on their arrival from Scotland; who, after staying a week, again set out on another voyage. I returned back to Beer, and employed myself in fishing, &c., until new year's day; when I called on Lord R., who was very angry with me for leaving the cutter, and told me if I was ill, he would have procured me a long leave of absence, but now he would do nothing more for me. I afterwards called upon several gentlemen to whom I was known; and they each gave me a new year's gift, which was the means of making myself and family very comfortable.

CHAPTER XVIII.

In February 1830, I sailed from Lyme as mate of a schooner bound for Topsham with half a cargo of wheat, from which place, having discharged our load, we proceeded to Exeter, and took in a cargo of manganese for Kilmarnock in Scotland. We sailed down the canal on the 10th of March with only three men and a boy, one of whom met with an accident that prevented him from being able to do any duty. On the 11th we sailed over Exmouth bar : I remained on deck myself for seven nights. On the 18th the wind was blowing very hard from the east, which obliged us to put in at Shields, where we staid four days, and got another hand instead of the one which was disabled, whom we left in the hospital. On the 22nd we proceeded on our voyage, and arrived at our destined port on the 28th, where we discharged our cargo, and I informed the captain that I wished to leave the vessel for the purpose of going to Banff to see my sons, upon which he paid me my wages, and gave me a good character.

I had a very fine passage to Spa in a smack, and proceeded from thence to Banff by land ; but my sons did not arrive till a few days afterwards, and I staid with them and shipped myself on board a little vessel of forty tons burden, carrying salmon to Aberdeen. I belonged to her two months, and then engaged in the herring fishery, in which I was very successful: when this was over, I embarked with my sons for London, where we arrived in the course of five days, and remained with them till they set out on another voyage, and then returned home to Beer in the latter end of August.

On the 4th of January, 1831, I observed a vessel about four leagues off from Beer with her colours flying for a pilot, upon which I got a boat and rowed off to her immediately, and found that she was a Dutchman which had sailed from Alexandria, and was bound to Amsterdam, but had mistaken the Portland light for that of the Gaskets. The captain agreed to give me fifteen pounds for carrying her into Exmouth harbour. The vessel being both leaky and foul, we rode quarantine five days, and then the Dutch agent paid me the sum for which I had stipulated, and I returned home.

In the month of September, as I was one day engaged in fishing about three leagues from land, I met with a very remarkable preservation from a watery grave; for as I was returning home towards evening, a violent gale of wind arose from the south-west, and a heavy sea broke over the boat, and washed a sail overboard, and carried me with it; but one of the men caught hold of the yard, by which means the sea hove me into the boat again, which was going at the rate of five or six knots an hour, so that we got home safely that night.

The latter end of this month I went to France, and

took in a cargo of goods, but lost the whole. On the
12th of November, in company with my son and two
men, I went to sea, and took up five-and-twenty kegs,
and about seven o'clock in the evening of the same
day we were chased and eventually captured by Lieutenant Buxton and his men (belonging to the Beer
preventive boat), who upon coming on board and finding nothing, hove the grappling irons overboard, but
all to no purpose; and yet, notwithstanding they
found only a piece of a rope about one fathom in length,
they took us into custody, and conveyed us to Lyme,
and the next day we were taken before the mayor and
the collector of the customs, when the preventive men
were examined, and we were remanded till an order
could be obtained from the board, which arrived on
the 19th, when we took our trial before the mayor and
one of the magistrates for the county. On this occasion we employed two attorneys, Mr. Flight and Mr.
Cann. The trial lasted from two till eight o'clock, and
although nothing was sworn to but the piece of rope
above mentioned, we were found guilty, and committed to Dorchester goal; whither we were conducted
by Lieutenant Buxton and a riding officer. In this
situation I was employed as a watchman by night,
and to look after the boys by day; and the manner
in which I discharged the duties belonging to both
these offices was such as to give great satisfaction
to the governor, the chaplain, and the doctor; and
the emolument arising from it tended very much to
lessen the hardships I had to endure. I remained in

confinement until February 1833, when through the
kind offices of Mr. Pinny, M. P. for Lyme, I once
more tasted the sweets of liberty.

In the March following, I again embarked on a
voyage to Cherburg, and returned with a cargo of spirits,
half of which was sunk, and lost; the remainder was
landed and concealed among the cliffs for three days
and nights, and at last conveyed away by daylight.

I made my next and last voyage to Cherburg in the
month of October in the same year, and on my return
sent a man on shore to procure assistance, but he was
unfortunately taken by some of the preventive men; I
therefore sunk the kegs myself, but lost the whole in
consequence of being laid up with a fit of the gout.

In the month of June, 1835, my son having sunk
some kegs, I went out in a boat under the pretence of
catching mackerel, about eleven o'clock in the morning,
and picked them up, and landed first one half and
then the other at a place called Charton bay, persons
being in readiness to receive them. Just as we were
returning we met two boats belonging to the coast
guard, going out for the purpose of securing them;
since which time two men have been stationed at the
place where we landed.

In the beginning of the month of January 1836, I
went to Torquay in a cart, where we took in twenty tubs
of brandy, and proceeded with it in the same convey-
ance to Newton Bushel; but some one having obtained
intelligence of the same, laid an information against
us, so that when we were about a mile out of Newton

Bushel, at ten o'clock at night, the officers came up on horseback, and one of them taking hold of the reins of the horse, said, " I seize this horse and cart in behalf of the king and myself." Upon hearing this I directly made my escape, but the man to whom the cart belonged was taken into custody, and conveyed to Exeter.

Thus ended my career as a smuggler,—a career which, however, it may be calculated to gratify a hardy and enterprising spirit, and to call forth all the latent energies of the soul, is fraught with difficulty and danger; in following which, many and various have been the expedients* to which I have had recourse, in

---

* .Probably a relation of a few of them would not be uninteresting to some of my readers.

On one occasion I had a goose on board, which the master who overhauled the vessel was very desirous of buying; but I was too well aware of the value of the stuffing to part with it, for instead of onions and sage, it consisted of fine lace.

About the same time I had stowed some valuable French silks in a tin box, which being soldered to prevent the water from getting in, while an officer was searching another part of the vessel, I contrived to throw it overboard, having previously attached to it a stone and a buoy, by which means I recovered the silks perfect and uninjured.

Having landed a cargo at Seaton Hole one dark night, I was going up the cliff with a keg at my back, when I had the ill-luck to stumble over an ass, which began to bray so horribly that together with the noise occasioned by my fall, woke an officer who was taking a nap below, in consequence of which he seized nearly forty kegs, being the whole of the cargo.

One day hearing that my son, whom I had sent to Seaton with a flagon of brandy, had been taken by a preventive man, I seized

order to escape detection, baffle pursuit, and elude the
vigilance of those indefatigable picaroons which every
where line our coasts. I have also experienced, as
may be seen in the foregoing narrative, the greatest
vicissitudes, my spirits having been alternately elated
by success, or depressed by misfortune; but in the
midst of the whole I never yielded to despair, for hope
was the pole-star which shed its cheering rays, and
illuminated my path in the darkest storms of adversity.

The last time I appeared in a public court was at
Exeter assizes, held in March 1836, as a witness in
behalf of my son, who was charged with having been
engaged with others in an affray on Budleigh Salterton
beach, which took place on the night of the first of
December, 1835; when William Noble Clay, and John
Bachelor, being officers in his majesty's customs, were
assaulted, maltreated, and obstructed in the discharge of their duty. The case excited considerable
interest; and notwithstanding numerous witnesses were
examined, who all testified to his being at Beer on the
night in question, and consequently not near the spot,
which is a distance of sixteen miles, he was found
guilty, and sentenced to seven years' transportation;
but through the kindness of some gentlemen of consequence, who narrowly investigated the case, and were
convinced of his innocence, several petitions, most
respectably signed, were sent to Lord John Russell,

---

a poker and ran out to effect his rescue, but I found that he had
escaped observation through climbing up into a tree.

To these I might add many more of a similar nature.

who presented them to the king, when he was graciously
pleased to grant him his royal pardon.

On this occasion I was cross-examined by Mr.
Sergeant Bompas; and as it caused a great deal of
amusement at the time, I have extracted the following
passages from a newspaper, which contained an account
of the trial. "I keep school at sea—fish for sole,
turbot and brill; any kind of fish that comes to hook."
"Which do you catch oftenest, soles or tubs?"—"Oh,
the devil a tub, (great laughter;) there are too many
picaroons going now-a-day." You have caught a good
many in your time?"—"Ah, plenty of it! I wish you
and I had as much of it as we could drink." (laughter.)
"You have kept school at home, and trained up your
son?"—"I have always trained him up in a regular
honourable way, larnt him the creed, the Lord's prayer,
and the ten commandments." "You don't find there,
Thou shalt not smuggle?"—"No, but I find there, Thou
shalt not bear false witness against thy neighbour."
"Nobody smuggles now-a-day?" — "Don't they,
though!"(laughter) "So these horses at Beer cannot go
above three or four miles an hour?"—"If you had not
better horses, you would never get to London. I seldom
ride a horse-back. If I do, I generally falls off
seven or eight times in a journey." (great laughter.)

Since I left off smuggling, I have been principally
engaged in fishing and piloting, but have lately entered
into an engagement for conveying the blue lias lime,
and the stone, for the harbour which is in contemplation
at Sidmouth. In the exercise of my profession as a
pilot, I have, under Divine Providence, been instru-

mental in saving many vessels from being wrecked. An instance of this kind occurred a short time ago, which is likely to occasion me some little inconvenience; for after I had succeeded in saving the vessel, a person who went on board, told the captain that I and those who had assisted me, were the very men who would rob him, which so roused my passions, that I instantly struck him a blow; and I have since been served with a summons to appear before the magistrates; but as I took no notice of that, I have received another.

The Smuggler gratefully acknowledges the kindness of the Right Hon. LORD ROLLE, who now allows him one shilling per week for life.

J. Harvey, Printer, Sidmouth.

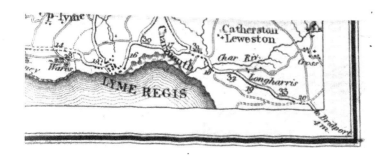